香港國際詩歌之夜 *2015*

INTERNATIONAL POETRY NIGHTS IN HONG KONG

詩歌與衝突

POETRY AND CONFLICT

編輯	**Editors**
北島	**Bei Dao**
陳嘉恩	**Shelby K. Y. Chan**
方梓勳	**Gilbert C. F. Fong**
柯夏智	**Lucas Klein**
馬德松	**Christopher Mattison**
宋子江	**Chris Song**

穆罕默德・貝尼斯 摩洛哥	**Mohammed Bennis** Morroco
陳黎 臺灣	**Chen Li** Taiwan
彼得・科爾 美國	**Peter Cole** USA
納捷宛・達爾維什 巴勒斯坦	**Najwan Darwish** Palestine
揚・米歇爾・埃斯比達列 法國	**Jean-Michel Espitallier** France
詹瑪・歌爾伽 西班牙	**Gemma Gorga** Spain
金惠順 韓國	**Kim Hyesoon** South Korea
科科瑟 緬甸	**ko ko thett** Burma
衣田・拉朗德 加拿大	**Étienne Lalonde** Canada
飲江 香港	**Lau Yee-ching** Hong Kong
尼古拉・馬茲洛夫 馬其頓	**Nikola Madzirov** Macedonia
艾棘・米索 以色列	**Agi Mishol** Israel
水田宗子 日本	**Noriko Mizuta** Japan
萊斯・馬雷 澳州	**Les Murray** Australia
費平樂 葡萄牙	**Fernando Pinto do Amaral** Portugal
格列勃・舒爾比亞科夫 俄羅斯	**Gleb Shulpyakov** Russia
宋琳 中國	**Song Lin** China
多和田葉子 日本	**Yoko Tawada** Japan
安妮・華曼 美國	**Anne Waldman** USA
王小妮 中國	**Wang Xiaoni** China
加桑・扎克坦 巴勒斯坦	**Ghassan Zaqtan** Palestine

序言

戰爭與和平，是人類歷史的永恆主題之一。自1945年到現在，七十年過去了，第二次世界大戰雖已結束，但局部戰爭從未間斷，侵佔領土、摧毀家園、屠殺平民，以及相伴的屈辱和精神創傷，觸目皆是。所謂現代文明的進步，往往以公理與自由的名義，弱肉強食，稱霸天下，全球化的權力與資本在繼續瓜分並統治著世界。

1989年成為歷史的轉折，東西方冷戰格局基本結束，但冷戰思維依然存在。更為複雜的是，自二十世紀末以來，以資本主導的全球化如洪流，鋪天蓋地，而互聯網革命帶來的信息爆炸，造成知識的碎片化和媒體的娛樂化，這一切徹底改變了舊的世界秩序，包括顛覆「傳統」的中產階級生活方式。與此同時，在物質浮華與娛樂洗腦的背後，令人觸目驚心的是侵略與戰亂，貧富日益懸殊，自然資源被掠奪，以及言論自由等條件的進一步惡化。

詩歌與衝突，是本屆2015年香港國際詩歌之夜的主題。

自古以來，詩歌總是以人類苦難為源泉，成為穿越黑暗趨向光明的驅動力。而今天，在文明、歷史、宗教和語言等諸多衝突中，詩歌何為？在錯亂紛雜的現世的病態幻象中，詩歌何為？在土地與天空閉合的神秘時刻，詩歌何為？在追溯精神的源流中叩問語言之門，詩歌何為？

北島

2015年8月10日於香港

Foreword

War and peace—one of humanity's eternal themes. From 1945 up to the present day, despite seventy years without another "world war," our world has never been free from war, invasion, destruction, slaughter, and the degradation and spiritual trauma that follow. What we call the progress of civilization is no more than the strong making fodder of the weak under the mantle of freedom, power and capital, in their endless quest for domination, globalizing only to carve up the world so as to better rule it.

The year 1989 was a historical turning point, but while the Cold War between East and West reached a kind of culmination, the Cold War mentality has continued unabated. Less straightforwardly, the sea swell of globalization led by capitalism since the end of the twentieth century has swallowed heaven and earth, and the internet revolution's information explosion has brought about both the fragmentation of knowledge and the transformation of the news media into amusement, thoroughly restructuring the old world order and overturning the "traditional" lifestyles of the middle class along with it. At the same time, on the flip side of material ostentatiousness and brainwashing by the media, we remain shocked at the continuation of hostility and upheaval, the growing disparity between rich and poor, the depletion of natural resources, and the progressive degradation of rights such as freedom of speech.

Poetry and Conflict: the theme for the 2015 International Poetry Nights in Hong Kong.

Since antiquity, poetry has been sourced in humanity's suffering, a driving force for the overcoming of darkness toward the light. Now, amid proposed conflicts between civilizations, histories, religions, and languages, what can poetry do? In the bedlam of the morbid fantasies of our world, what can poetry do? In this moment of mystery when land and air are collapsing, what can poetry do? In retracing the source and course of our spiritual knocking at language's door, what can poetry do?

Bei Dao
August 10, 2015, Hong Kong

目錄 Contents

香港國際詩歌之夜 2015
INTERNATIONAL POETRY NIGHTS IN HONG KONG

穆罕默德・貝尼斯，1948 年生於摩洛哥費斯市，現代阿拉伯文詩歌界最重要的詩人之一。1970 年代起至今，貝尼斯已出版三十多本書籍（包括詩歌、評論、散文、翻譯、摩洛哥詩歌研究專著，以及現代阿拉伯文詩歌研究專著），並不時在阿拉伯世界各大報章雜誌發表詩歌和評論，作品譯本也見刊於歐洲、美國和日本。貝尼斯為現代阿拉伯語詩歌作出了巨大貢獻，在當今阿拉伯文化界中享有極高地位。其詩作曾被翻譯成法文、西班牙文、意大利文、土耳其文、馬其頓文，以及德文等多國語言。此外，貝尼斯亦曾將法文詩歌譯成阿拉伯文，其譯作包括《擲骰：史提芬・馬拉美詩選》(2007)。

Mohammed Bennis is one of the most important poets of modern Arabic poetry. He was born in Fez, Morocco, in 1948. He contributes energetically to modern Arabic poetry and has been widely respected in the Arab world since the 1970s. The author of more than thirty titles (poetry, prose, essays, and translations, among them, fifteen poetry collections, and studies on Moroccan poetry and modern Arabic poetry), Bennis has published in numerous newspapers and reviews all over the Arab world. Some of his poems and texts have been translated and published in collected works, reviews and newspapers in Europe, the United States and Japan. From 1995, published translations of his poetry collections and books have appeared in French, Spanish, Italian, Turkish, Macedonian and German. He has also translated French works into Arabic including *A Throw of the Dice: Poems of Stéphane Mallarmé* (2007).

穆罕默德·貝尼斯

MOHAMMED BENNIS

ظنون

لهَذي الظنونِ التي
نَسْتضيءُ بها
لهَذي المَنافي التي التأَمَتْ
بينَها
نُحدّد لونَ الأثرْ
وَننثُرهُ
بجَعاً
وننثُرهُ
موْجةً
أوْ حجَرْ

猜想

因為這些
啟迪我們的猜想
因為這些
相互交織的流亡地
我們劃定足跡的顏色
把它播撒成
　　　一隻鵜鶘
　　播撒成
　　　一朵浪濤
　　　　或一粒石子

(唐珺　譯)

Doubts

With these doubts
that illuminates us

With these exiles
that interweave

We heighten the colour
of the trace
and we scatter it
　　　　pelicans
　　scatter it
　　　　wave
　　　　　or stone

(Translated by James Kirkup)

طيْــش

لا تسْألوهُ
عَنِ
المَسَالكِ
رُبّما
ثقُلتْ عَلـيْهِ
ليُونةُ الأغْصَانِ
في أفُقٍ يُهدّدُ صمْــتهُ

لا تَسألوهُ
عَنِ
المَهالكِ
رُبّما
عَبرتْ إليْه نهايةُ
مِنْ شــوْقهِ

لا تَسْألوهُ
عنِ
المَناسكِ
إنّهُ
طيشُ رمَى
بدمَائـهِ
وانقَادَ للنّسْــيَانْ

輕率

你們不要問他
關於道路的事
或許
枝條的柔韌
把他壓得太重
那一片天際，為他的沉默所脅迫

你們不要問他
關於險惡的事
或許
他終結的渴望
正對他潸然淚下

你們不要問他
關於
修行的事
那是輕率
放棄了自己的血液
順從了遺忘的引領

(唐珺　譯)

Frivolity

Don't ask him anything
about the pathways
perhaps he feels the weight
of the branches' lightsomeness
below the horizon threatened by silence

Don't ask him anything
about the dangers
the ending of his passion
perhaps
has its origin in him

Don't ask him anything
about the
rites
he is frivolous
he casts away his own blood
and leaps towards forgetting

(Translated by James Kirkup)

لقــاء

تقدّمْ يا شبيهيَ في المَنامِ رأيتهُ يدنُو من الصّلصَالِ
أزرقَ ثم ينفخُ في رنينيَ يومَ عادُوا شاحبينَ بصرْخةٍ
ممّا تبقّى منْ فوانيسِ الزيارةِ هذه الصّحراءُ نصْحبُها
إلى ليْلٍ تدافعتِ النجُومُ على بُرودتهِ حُميّا الضّوء
بعْثرْنا مَعادنَها لتكْتسيَ البَسيطةُ بالغناءْ

فلأيّ
رابيةٍ
سَنصْعدُ يا دَليليَ
في انْكشَافِ الصّمتِ بينَ حَدائقِ الأمْواتِ وسّعْ سلْسبيلَ
يديْكَ جوّفْ وردةَ التّكْوينِ يعْبُرني أنينُ المُبحرينَ من
الضّفافِ إلى الضّفافِ
أتلكَ
عائلتي
تذكّرُني
بشعْشعةِ المَنافي

يَسْتعيدُ
تلوّنُ الحَصبَاتِ
وحْدتَهُ
يَسوقُ دمُ المَشيئةِ لانهايَتهُ
يرتّلُ عُشْبَهُ
نهْرُ
المَساءْ

遇見

另一個我，快來我的夢裏。我看見他
從藍色的粘土中走近
注入我的共振裏。
那日他們憔悴歸來，
在所剩無幾的旅行燈籠裏嘶吼
我們伴隨沙漠來到黑夜
那裏的星辰把光的灼熱傾倒在寒冷裏，
我們把金屬碎片播撒，為純樸披上歌唱

　　哪個
　　山丘
　　我們將攀爬
　　啊，我的嚮導

在亡者公園顯露的寂靜裏，
快充沛你手間的醴泉，
快掘出創世的玫瑰，
水手們的呻吟穿透我
從一片海岸抵達另一片。
　　那是不是
　　我的家庭
　　讓我想起
流亡地的閃光

　　小石子的華彩
　　恢復了
　　它的孤寂。
　　期望的血液驅使它永恆，
　　夜的
　　河流
　　吟詠著綠草的頌歌。

（唐珺　譯）

Encounter

You fellow man advance In my sleep I've seen him He approaches the blue clay Then he blows upon my remains re-echoing That day the funereal visitors returned all pale in the cry of the last lanterns we accompany the desert towards night The stars there are toppling in the cold we have dispersed the source of light and of its ardour so that song may cover the earth

Towards
What dune
My
guide
are we going?

In the unveiling of silence in the gardens of the dead Let the pure waters of your hands be more abundant Dig the flower of genesis The moans of the navigators pierce me from one bank to the other

Is it
My family
That reminds me
the radiance of exiles

The colour
of little pebbles
again harvests
its solitude
The blood of the will conducts its infinity

The river
of evening
sings the grasses' psalms

(Translated by James Kirkup)

عَمَـى

يعْلُو بيَ هذا الحبْرُ إلى نفَسي
يعْلُو بيَ مُنتَصراً
ثمّ إلى حيثُ يُراودُ عيْنيَ
يعْلُو
حتّى تنْشأَ في
غَفْلةِ حُمّايَ
مراتيجُ
ومواسمُ حنّاءٍ
ومنازلُ منْ ليلِ الرّقصاتِ
إلى
ليْلِ الرّقصاتْ
ويكونُ النّخْلُ قريباً من خُطواتٍ
نسيَتْ صاحبَها
ومشيئَتَها

تحتَ الصّمتِ فجَأتُ
صريراً
دائرةَ الشّمعِ تذوبْ
وفراشاً
ينْهضُ من لطْختهِ
وطُيوراً قادتْني
بتوزُّعهَا
لعَمَايْ

盲

這墨汁將我抬升至呼吸的高度
它威風地將我抬升
抵達那迷幻了我雙眼的高度
向上抬升
直至我迷糊的狂熱
誕生了
門閂、
紋身時節、
和家園，從舞蹈的夜
通往
舞蹈的夜。
那臨近椰棗樹的步伐
忘記了它的主人、
和它的祈願。

沉默之下，突現
嘎吱的聲響
蠟燭圈在融化
蝴蝶
從墨點中驚醒
鳥兒的紛飛
把我引向
盲

(唐珺　譯)

Blindness

This ink transports me to the heights of my breath
transports me there in triumph
it rises and my eye falls in love
rises to where my unconscious fever
unleashes disasters
festivals of henna
night that leads
to other nights of dance
the palm tree is near then
to the lost steps
neither god nor master
silence
and under the silence
a cracking surprised
like a seal that is breaking
ink stain wherein awake butterflies
word from which birds launch out
and their flight conducts me
towards blindness

(Translated by James Kirkup)

صَمْت

هذَا الصمتُ في أُفُق المكانْ
يعلُو
منَ الحَجرِ الدّفيءِ

لا شيْءَ
يخدشُ مستقرَّ أصَابعي
وهواءُ ليْلتنا
تقدّمَ طائعاً
غمرتهُ سلسلةُ منَ الصّفصافِ
رائحةُ القرنفُلِ
وانحناءُ الموجِ في دعَةٍ

هنا سنُقيمُ للضّحكاتُ
مسْكنَها
ونرحلُ في مُعاشَرة انفلاتِ الضوْءِ
منْ
أفُقِ المَكانْ

沉默

這沉默
從溫暖的石頭升起
上升至土地的天際

沒有甚麼
能抓破我手指的沉穩
我們夜晚的空氣
順從地前行
浸淫在排排柳樹、
丁香、
和波濤和緩的漣漪裏。

在這裏，我們將為笑靨
建起居所
我們將離去
伴隨飛速的光
從土地的天際出發

（唐珺　譯）

Silence

This silence rises from the warm
stone
rises to the horizon

Nothing
troubles the touch of fingers
The breeze of our night
Advances with docility
a wave of poplars submerges it
night-scenting stocks perfuming
the subdued rumblings of the eddies

Here we construct with laughter
a dwelling place and we
shall depart in company with
the flight of the radiance
that flows from the horizon

(Translated by James Kirkup)

دنَـــس

حينَ أُلاقي جسَدي الطّافحَ منْ بللِ الشّيْءِ الخَالصْ
وتجَاويفِ الكلمَاتْ
يتهيّأُ لي أنّي أتوضّأُ بالصّمْتِ
المَمْسُوسِ
وَبالدّنسِ النّشّويّْ
تنْحلّ اللّطخاتْ
في مَاء الرّغْبةِ
ينْسلُّ سديمُ كانَ يقولْ
لا تَكْتُبْ

污穢

當我遇見我的身體
浮出純粹物體的濕潤裏
浮出詞語的內腔，
準備好清潔自己
用可觸的沉默
用醉人的污穢。
污濁消融在
欲望之水裏
薄霧在褪去
它當時在對我説
不要寫

（唐珺　譯）

Impurity

This is my body I meet it
It emerges all wet from the pure thing
and from the hollow of words
I watch myself at my absolutions
haunted by silence
with ecstatic purity
The defilements are diluted
in the waters of desire
A nothingness
that was telling me
Do not write
is withdrawing

(Translated by James Kirkup)

陳黎，原名陳膺文，1954 年生，臺灣花蓮人，臺灣師範大學英語系畢業。被視為「當今中文詩界最能創新且令人驚喜的詩人之一」，著有十四本詩集，且是多產的散文作者和譯者。與妻子張芬齡合譯有二十餘種詩集，包括普拉絲、奚尼、聶魯達、帕斯、辛波絲卡、特朗斯特羅默及與謝野晶子等人的作品。曾獲國家文藝獎、臺灣文學獎等諸多獎項，是一年一度在花蓮舉行的「太平洋詩歌節」策劃人。2005 年獲選「臺灣當代十大詩人」。2012 年獲邀代表臺灣參加倫敦奧林匹克詩歌節。2014 年受邀參加美國愛荷華大學「國際寫作計劃」。

Chen Li was born in Hualien, Taiwan, in 1954, and graduated from the English Department of National Taiwan Normal University. Regarded as one of the most innovative and exciting poets writing in Chinese today, he is a prolific prose writer and translator as well as the author of fourteen books of poetry. With his wife Chang Fen-ling, he has translated over twenty volumes of poetry into Chinese, including the works of Sylvia Plath, Seamus Heaney, Pablo Neruda, Octavio Paz, Wisława Szymborska, Tomas Tranströmer, and Akiko Yosano. The recipient of many awards, such as the National Award for Literature and Arts and the Taiwan Literature Award, he is the organizer of the annual Pacific Poetry Festival in his hometown. In 2005, he was listed as one of the "Top Ten Contemporary Poets of Taiwan." In 2012, he represented Taiwan at Poetry Parnassus, the Olympic Poetry Festival held in London. In 2014, he was invited to participate in the International Writing Program at the University of Iowa.

陳黎

CHEN LI

二月

槍聲在黃昏的鳥群中消失

失蹤的父親的鞋子
失蹤的兒子的鞋子

在每一碗清晨的粥裏走回來的腳步聲
在每一盆傍晚的洗臉水裏走回來的腳步聲

失蹤的母親的黑髮
失蹤的女兒的黑髮

在異族的統治下反抗異族
在祖國的懷抱裏被祖國強暴

芒草。薊花。曠野。吶喊

失蹤的秋天的日曆
失蹤的春天的日曆

February

Gunshots die away among the birds at dusk

Shoes of missing fathers
Shoes of missing sons

Footsteps returning to every morning bowl of porridge
Footsteps returning to the water of every evening washbasin

Missing black hair of mothers
Missing black hair of daughters

Rebellion against foreigners under a foreign regime
Ravished by the fatherland while in its embrace

Reeds. Thistles. Wilderness. Outcries

Missing calendars of autumn
Missing calendars of spring

(Translated by Chang Fen-ling)

獵像者

—— 紀念凱文・卡特

如果遠方有戰爭，持步槍、長矛
斧頭的黑棋，和全副武裝的白棋
在街頭肉搏混戰，如果一顆棋子
倒地，哀嚎，鮮血四濺
以相機為槍的獵者啊，你如何
快步移位，停止呼吸，扣扳機般
按下快門，在死亡尚未離席前補上
一槍，及時獵取它最動人的圖像

如果遠方有飢餓，赤裸乾癟的人類
相擁於荒野，等候血與淚的聖餐
餵養他們的軀體，如果一名女童
頹然倒下，頭觸大地，一隻兀鷹
在她身後虎視眈眈等待屍肉
以慈悲為懷的獵者啊，你如何
緩緩移步，強忍自責，小心不驚動
覓食的兀鷹，不破壞畫面的完整
為了給世人真實而哀痛的藝術

如果遠方有戰爭，道德與藝術
良知與職責，如果一塊活生生的
腐肉上死亡的蒼蠅與美的蒼蠅
同時飛聚，坐在書房裏閱覽世界的
詩人啊，你如何揮動刻度迥異的
現實與美感的拍子，如何絞緊苦難
與熱情的發條，讓果實鬆弛流出
汁液，你如何以語字的圖像沖洗
悲劇的圖像，如何以矛盾的悲憫
化解悲憫的矛盾？

註：
凱文・卡特 (Kevin Carter)，一九六〇年生，南非攝影記者。一九九四年五月，以一張即將餓斃為兀鷹所食的蘇丹女童照片（刊載於一九九三年三月《紐約時報》）獲頒普立茲新聞特寫攝影獎。得獎後卡特頗遭批判，謂其以別人的不幸換取鏡頭。一九九四年七月，卡特以一氧化碳自殺身亡，遺言：「很遺憾，生命終究是苦多於樂。」

The Image Hunter

—In memory of Kevin Carter

If there is a war far away, and the black chess pieces
carry rifles, spears, and axes to fight hand to hand against
the fully armed white chess pieces on the street,
if a pawn falls and wails, blood splashing,
how will you, hunter with a camera for a gun,
quickly reposition, hold your breath, and close the shutter
like pulling a trigger to take another shot before
death departs, to hunt in time the most moving image?

If there is hunger far away, and naked emaciated people
embracing each other in the wilderness, awaiting the Holy
Communion of blood and tears to feed their bodies,
if a girl falls, weakly, head to earth, a vulture
above her waiting with cruel greed for her corpse,
oh merciful hunter, how will you slowly
reposition, restrain your guilt, cautious not to
frighten the vulture and spoil the picture,
so you can present the world your true and grievous art?

If there is a war far away, morality and art, conscience
and duty, if the mosquito of death and the mosquito
of beauty meet simultaneously on a living lump of
rotting flesh, how will you, poets in your studies reading
about the world, wave your differently graded swats
of reality and aesthetics, how will you wind the springs
of suffering and passion, to slacken fruit enough to ooze
juice, how will you develop the tragic images with
word pictures, how to reconcile contradictory compassion
with compassionate contradiction?

(Translated by Chang Fen-ling)

Translator's Note:
Kevin Carter was a South African photojournalist born in 1960. In May 1994, he won the Pulitzer Prize for feature photography for an image of a Sudanese girl on the verge of dying of starvation and being eaten by vultures (printed in *The New York Times*, March 1993). After the award Carter was criticized for capturing the scene at the cost of others' misfortune. In July, 1994, Carter died from carbon monoxide poisoning. His suicide note read, "I'm really, really sorry. The pain of life overrides the joy to the point that joy does not exist."

小宇宙

我等候，我渴望你：
一粒骰子在夜的空碗裏
企圖轉出第七面
*
寂寥冬日裏的重大
事件：一塊耳屎
掉落在書桌上
*
所有夜晚的憂傷都要在白日
轉成金黃的稻穗，等候
另一個憂傷的夜晚收割
*
雲霧小孩的九九乘法表：
山乘山等於樹，山乘樹等於
我，山乘我等於虛無……
*
在不斷打破世界紀錄之後
我們孤寂的鉛球選手，一舉
把自己的頭擲出去
*
一顆痣因肉體的白
成為一座島：我想念
你衣服裏波光萬頃的海
*
婚姻物語：一個衣櫃的寂寞加
一個衣櫃的寂寞等於
一個衣櫃的寂寞
*
爭鳴：
0歲的老蟬教0歲的
幼蟬唱「生日快樂」
*
人啊，來一張
存在的寫真：囚

Microcosmos

I wait and long for you:
a rolling die in the empty bowl of night
attempting to turn on a seventh side

*

A great event on a desolate
winter day: ear wax
drops onto the desk

*

All the sorrow of night will turn into golden
ears of rice by daylight, to be
reaped by another sorrowful night

*

Multiplication table for children of cloud and fog:
mountain times mountain equals tree, mountain times tree
equals me, mountain times me equals nothingness…

*

Having consistently broken world records
our lonely shot-putter throws his head out
in one put

*

White skin makes a mole
an isle: I miss the glistening
vast ocean within your clothes

*

A story of marriage: a closet of loneliness plus
a closet of loneliness equals
a closet of loneliness

*

Chirping competition:
zero-year-old old cicadas teach zero-year-old
baby cicadas to sing Happy Birthday

*

Ah human, come and
take a selfie: encaged

(Translated by Chang Fen-ling)

北方

北方在我夢中草原豎立起一座空中捺缽[1]。那年輕的契丹王，啣著一枝玫瑰，回轉快馬，徒手扯下了兩名節度使的氣節和器度，飛鴿傳書，要長安城裏的帝王把最小、最美的公主嫁給他。崇勇惜美的帝王不及三思即應許了他，要求以三百瓶其色瑩白，其香濃郁的契丹玫瑰油為聘禮。契丹的使者們，興奮地迎回了芬芳公主—— 他們的新王后—— 以及她的嫁妝。她的嫁妝就是她自己。她身上未曾滴任何玫瑰油，但一股莫名其狀的芬芳隨她來到契丹王的宮帳，彷彿來自天上，而非塵世。那香味不只是嗅覺的，還是視覺的，暈染過懸掛帳內的〈秋林群鹿圖〉和〈丹楓呦鹿圖〉，讓兩幅畫和整個帳內氤氳著明亮斑斕的秋色。我不知道宮帳甚麼時候變成空中林園，只聽到侍女們吹著觱篥、笛、笙，彈著琵琶、箏、箜篌，而契丹王居中吟唱，與新娘、群臣隨音樂飛昇，在我草原夢中。

註：

1. 捺缽，契丹語的譯音，意為契丹主巡狩時的行營、行宮、行在所。

The North

The North erected a hanging imperial tent above the grasslands in my dream. The young Khitan King, a rose between his lips, turned his galloping horse around and, with bare hands, tore off the courage and grandeur of two Chinese provincial governors. Pigeons carried his message requeting the Emperor in Chang-an to pick the youngest and fairest princess to be his bride. Without a second thought the valiant and beauty-worshiping emperor granted his request, asking for three hundred bottles of crystal white and fragrant Khitan rose attar in return. The envoys of Khitan escorted Princess Aroma—their new queen—along with her dowry. Her dowry was herself. Not a single drop of rose attar on her body, an indescribable aroma followed her into the imperial tent, as if from heaven, not the world of dust. The aroma was not only olfactory, but visual, and spread over *Herd of Deer in an Autumn Forest* and *Deer among Red Maples* in the tent, bathing the two paintings in the bright and gorgeous hues of autumn. I don't know when the imperial tent became a hanging garden; I just heard maidservants playing the Tatar horn, the bamboo flute, the sheng-pipes, the pipa-lute, the zither, and the konghou-harp. Singing to the music, the Khitan King rose to the air with his bride and officials in my dream of the grasslands.

(Translated by Chang Fen-ling)

彼得・科爾，最近發表的詩集為《影響之發明》（2014），譯作包括《卡巴拉詩歌：猶太傳統的神秘詩歌》（2012）、《詩之夢：西班牙的希伯來文詩歌（950–1492）》（2007），以及阿赫朗・沙布泰、塔哈・穆罕穆德・阿里、尤爾・霍夫曼等人的文學作品。科爾曾獲「國家藝術獎金」、「古根漢基金會獎」、「國家猶太圖書獎（詩歌類）」、「筆會翻譯獎（詩歌類）」、「美國藝文學會文學獎」、「麥克阿瑟獎」等。科爾常年往返於耶路撒冷和美國康納狄克州紐黑文城。

Peter Cole's most recent book of poems is *The Invention of Influence* (New Directions, 2014). His many volumes of translation include *The Poetry of Kabbalah: Mystical Verse from the Jewish Tradition* (Yale, 2012) and *The Dream of the Poem: Hebrew Poetry from Muslim and Christian Spain, 950–1492* (Princeton, 2007), as well as poetry and fiction by Aharon Shabtai, Taha Muhammad Ali, Yoel Hoffmann, and others. Cole has received numerous honours for his work, including fellowships from the National Endowment for the Arts and the Guggenheim Foundation, the National Jewish Book Award for Poetry, the PEN Translation Award for Poetry, and an Award in Literature from the American Academy of Arts and Letters. He was named a MacArthur Fellow in 2007. He divides his time between Jerusalem and New Haven, Connecticut.

彼得・科爾

PETER COLE

On Being Partial

I'm partial to what's possible,
he thought— not the ineffable,
distant, devoid of insistence
and temperament that tampers,
or tramples
                Not the impersonal,
but that which hovers here
between the "I" of the opening
and the "us" of your possible listening
now, or in the imperfect
tense and tension of what
in fact articulates the eternal
That abstract revelation
and slippery duration
to which, it seems, I'm given
and because of which I'm never
finished with anything, as though living
itself were an endless translation

談偏愛

我對有可能發生的特別偏愛，
他想——不要說不出的，
冷淡無情，易於放棄
及按捺怒氣或蹂躪
性情的
　　　不要客觀的，
要那徘徊於這裏的，
位於「我」的開端
與「我們」聆聽之間，
或是於未完成
時態與張力中
表達永恆的
抽象的揭示
及含糊的時間
這一切我都擁有
亦正因此我永遠
難於完成任何東西，生活
猶如是永無止境的翻譯

（何麗明　譯）

News That Stays

"It's a multiday process…
                    Under stress,
officially MIA, with a mission. Friendly fire.
  That's not your question?
    I have a good *answer* for it.

Sorry, but we just can't discuss that,
and I can't even discuss why we can't discuss it.

Let me walk you through that decision. Unhindered:

Elite
              Republican
                              Guard.

Cut it off and then kill it. In my mind's eye . . . a thousand
    points of light. If you've
      got a hammer, *find* a nail.

  What the vulnerabilities are.

I'm not trying to
gaff the question. That's a service prerogative.

To classify these folks as prisoners of war.

…

Could you tell us, Pete, if the slick will spread
  and poison all the waters in the region? I
  don't think we have a good feeling for that.

Something has happened to his country
  that he doesn't want us to see.

A daisy cutter, to soften-up the troops.
Just ripple off . . . into infinity!
  A new order. Tel Aviv . . . a
crematorium. We haven't yet reached, I think,
      a point of diminishing

returns. By popular demand. Mr. Ambassador,
thank you very much for your time. My pleasure."

—*The Gulf War, 1991*

逗留的新聞

「那過程長達數天……
在壓力下
他放棄任務。誤傷隊友。
那不是你問的問題？
但我可以提供一個好的答案。

抱歉，但我們實在不能談論那事，
也不能談論我們為何不能談論那事。

讓我告訴你那決定是如何通過的。毫無保留的：

精鋭
共和國
衛隊。

把它剪斷，然後殺掉。在我眼裏……千
點光凝聚。
若你擁有一個錘子，就應找到那枚釘子。

了解他方的弱點。

我並無意
迴避你的問題。那是服務的特權。

把他們標為戰俘。
……

請告訴我們，彼得，石油會否覆蓋
及毒化所有沿海區域？我們
對這事很不是味兒。

他的國家發生了事
但他不想我們目睹。

投射滾球，削弱對方的軍隊。
像漣漪般擴散……無盡無窮！
新秩序。特拉維夫……
火葬場。我們還未到達
收益遞減

的地步。徇眾要求。大使先生，
很感謝你的時間。這是我的榮幸。」

—— 波斯灣戰爭，1991

（何麗明　譯）

Coexistence:
A Lost and Almost Found Poem

And the Levites shall speak, and say
unto all the men of Israel, with a loud voice:

Over the border the barrier winds,
devouring orchards of various kinds.

Cursed be he that taketh away
the landmark of his neighbor.
And all the people shall say, Amen.

The road was blocked in a battle of wills—
as the lame and sightless trudged through the hills.

Cursed be he that maketh the blind
to go astray in the way.
And all the people shall say, Amen.

The army has nearly written a poem:
You'll now need a permit just to stay home.

Cursed be he that perverteth the justice
due to the stranger (in Scripture).
And all the people shall say, Amen.

Taken away—in the dead of night—
by the secret policeman, who might be a Levite.

Cursed be he that turneth to smite
his neighbor in secret murder.
And all the people shall say, Amen—

as peace is sought through depredation,
living together in separation.

Cursed be he that confirmeth not
the words of this law—to do them.
And all the people shall say, Amen.

同存：
一首失而幾乎復得的詩

利未人要向
以色列眾人高聲説：

越過邊界障礙重重，
繁種的果園被吞沒。

詛咒那奪去
*　　鄰人地標的。*
眾人道，阿門。

鬥爭中道路被封閉——
跛子瞎子跋涉上山。

詛咒那引致
*　　盲人迷路的。*
眾人道，阿門。

軍隊將完成一詩歌：
留家者要獲得許可。

詛咒那以外人為名
*　　（經文所示）而毀滅正義的。*
眾人道，阿門。

被奪去——夜闌人靜時——
密探可能是利未人。

詛咒那捶打
*　　及暗殺鄰人的。*
眾人道，阿門——

要和平得先歷破壞，
於分裂間尋求共存。

詛咒那不認同
*　　這定律——但奉行的。*
眾人道，阿門。

（何麗明　譯）

Israel Is

Israel is he, or she, who wrestles
with God—call him what you will,

not some goon (with a rabbi and gun)
in a pre-fab home on a biblical hill.

以色列是

以色列是他，是她，與神
拚鬥——無論你怎樣稱呼他，

在那之前不是無賴（引述教士或手持武器）
於《聖經》提到的山上建設活動房屋並定居

（何麗明　譯）

納捷宛・達爾維什，阿拉伯文年輕詩人，其成就在同輩中尤為突出。達爾維什1978 年生於耶路撒冷，那年剛好是他的父母被趕出耶路撒冷西部的三十週年。在約旦安曼學習法律，當上律師不久後，他即轉投文學事業，在巴勒斯坦國內兩本文化雜誌任編輯一職，並在2006 至2012 年期間為黎巴嫩當地大報《Al-Akhbar》撰寫文化評論。達爾維什曾多次擔任公共藝術項目組織成員及顧問，包括巴勒斯坦文學節。2009 年，他在耶路撒冷成立了一家文學出版社，目前則正在籌辦一份泛阿拉伯世界的報紙，並會擔任文藝版主編。達爾維什於2000 年出版自己的第一本詩集，此後揚名阿拉伯世界，他的詩已給翻譯成十五種語言在世界各地出版。2009 年，達爾維什獲貝魯特文學節選為「39 歲以下39 位最佳阿拉伯文作家」之一。他現居耶路撒冷。

Najwan Darwish, one of the foremost Arabic language poets of his generation, was born in Jerusalem in 1978, exactly thirty years after his family was exiled from their home in the western part of the city. Shortly after studying in Amman, Jordan, and becoming a lawyer, he decided to give up law and devote himself to literature. He then worked as the editor of two cultural magazines in Palestine and was a cultural critic for the prominent Lebanese newspaper *Al-Akhbar* from 2006 to 2012. He has also been an organizer and advisor for many public arts projects, among them the Palestine Festival of Literature. In 2009, he founded a literary press in Jerusalem, and is currently involved in establishing a new pan-Arab newspaper, where he is to become the chief editor for the arts and culture section. Since the publication of his first collection in 2000, Darwish's poetry has been acclaimed across the Arab world and has been translated into fifteen languages. In 2009, he was on the Hay Festival Beirut's list of the "best 39 Arab authors under the age of 39." He currently resides in Jerusalem.

納捷宛 · 達爾維什

NAJWAN DARWISH

حتى في الحرب

خطر لي أَن أَنظر لقسمي الأَسفل حيث الوجع
ولكن للحظةٍ ردعتُ نفسي خشية أَلا أَجد جزءاً من جسدي
واصلتُ هبوط الأَدراج ومعي الجزء المفقود من جسدي
وها أَنا أَدخل السرير بجسدي الناقص (أَيضاً دون أَن أَنظر)
ولا يهم الآن أَين وقعت الخسارة
ولا يجدي أَن أَتذكّر كيف وأَين أُصبتُ

حتّى في الحرب كنتُ عابراً.

即使在戰爭中

我突然想低頭看看自己疼痛的下半身
一時間又制止自己，唯恐找不見身體的一部分
我帶著這丟失的部分，一路走下樓梯
又拖著殘缺的身體，爬上床去（依然不忍細看）
我已經不在乎究竟殘缺了何處
就算記得是何時怎樣受傷，也於事無補

即使在戰爭中，我仍舊是匆匆過客

(牛子牧　譯)

Even in War

I considered looking at my lower half
where I could feel the pain
but held back for the moment, fearing
not to find some part of me
I kept on down the stairs, my missing part
still with me, and here I am
climbing into bed with my wanting body
(still not looking), and it no longer matters
where the damage is, and it will do no good
to remember how I was wounded

Even in war, I was just a passer-by

(Translated by Kareem James Abu-Zeid)

نوم في غزّة

سأَنام يا فادوس مثلما ينام الناس والطائراتُ تَضْرِبُ
والهواءُ يتمزّق
كاللَّحم الحيّ
سأَحلم إذن بالخيانات
مثلما يحلم الذين ينامون والطائرات تَضْرِبُ

سأَستيقظ في الظهيرة لأَسأَل الراديو ـــــ مثلما يسأَلُ الناس:
هل توقّف القصفُ؟ وكم صار عدد الذين قُتلوا؟

لكنّ مأَساتي يا فادوس
أَنّ الناس نوعان:
الذين يُلقون عذاباتهم وخطاياهم على قوارع الطُرق ليناموا
والذين يجمعون عذابات الناس وخطاياهم على هيئة صلبان
ويسيرون بها في شوارع بابل وغزّة وبيروت
وهم يصيحون: هل مِنْ مزيد
هل مِنْ مزيد

قبل سنتين كنتُ في شوارع "الضاحية الجنوبيّة" أَجرُّ صليباً بحجم العمارات
لكن، من يحمل اليوم صليباً عن ظهر مُتْعَبٍ في أورشليم؟

الأَرض ثلاثة مسامير
والرحمة مِطْرَقة
اضرب يا ربّ
اضرب مع الطائرات

هل مِنْ مزيد؟

(كانون الأوّل 2009)

沉睡在加沙

我將和其他人一樣沉睡，法多[1]，枕著飛機的轟鳴
和空氣的撕裂
——就像鮮活的血肉四散橫飛
於是我將夢見背叛
就像其他枕著飛機的轟鳴沉睡的人一樣

我將在晌午時分醒來，和其他人一同詢問收音機：
轟炸停止了嗎？又有多少人已經死去？

可是啊法多，我的悲劇在於
人分為兩類：
有的把自己的痛苦和錯誤扔到路口，便可回家安睡
還有的撿回別人的痛苦和錯誤做成十字架，背起來走上巴比倫、
　　加沙和貝魯特的街頭
一邊吆喝著：還有嗎？
　　　　　　還有嗎？

兩年以前，我在南郊街頭拖著樓房般巨大的十字架
而今，誰又在耶路撒冷用疲憊的雙肩背負這十字架？

這世界是三顆釘子
而慈悲是一把錘子
砸吧，主啊
和轟炸機一起砸吧
還有嗎？

2009年12月

(牛子牧　譯)

譯註：
1. 法多(Fado)是葡萄牙文，代表「命運」；也代表了悲傷和憂鬱的歌聲。

Sleeping in Gaza

Fado,[1] I'll sleep like people do
when shells are falling
and the sky is torn like living flesh
I'll dream, then, like people do
when shells are falling:
I'll dream of betrayals

I'll wake at noon and ask the radio
the questions people ask of it:
Is the shelling over?
How many were killed?

But my tragedy, Fado,
is that there are two types of people:
those who cast their suffering and sins
into the streets so they can sleep
and those who collect the people's suffering and sins
mold them into crosses, and parade them
through the streets of Babylon and Gaza and Beirut
all the while crying
Are there any more to come?
Are there any more to come?

Two years ago I walked through the streets
of Dahieh, in southern Beirut
and dragged a cross
as large as the wrecked buildings
But who today will lift a cross
from the back of a weary man in Jerusalem?

The earth is three nails
and mercy a hammer:
Strike, Lord
Strike with the planes

Are there any more to come?

December 2009

(Translated by Kareem James Abu-Zeid)

Translator's Note:

1. The Portuguese word for "fate"; fado is also a popular form of mournful and melancholic singing, evoking loss or resignation to one's fate.

باص الكوابيس إلى صبرا وشاتيلا

رأَيتهم يضعون خالاتي في أَكياس بلاستيك سوداء
وفي زوايا الأَكياس تتجمّع دماؤهنّ الحارة
(لكن أَنا ليس لي خالات)
عرفت أَنّهم قد قتلوا ناتاشا ــــ إبنتي التي في الثالثة
(لكن أَنا ليس لي ابنة)
قيل لي إنّهم اغتصبوا زوجتي قبل أَن يجرّوا جسمها على الدرج
ويتركوه في الشارع
(لكن أَنا لم أَتزوّج)
لا شكّ هذه نظّارتي التي تحطّمت تحت البسطار
(لكن أَنا لا أَلبس نظّارة !)
...
كنتُ نائماً في بيت والديّ أَحلم بالسفر إلى بيتها، وحين استيقظت:
رأيت إخوتي
يتدلّون
من سقف كنيسة القيامة.
كان الربّ يقول من الشفقة: هذا أَلمي أَنا.
وكنت أَستجمع كبرياء المُعلَّقين وأَقول: لا بل هذا أَلمنا!
...

الأَلم يضيء ويصير أَحبّ إليّ من كوابيسي.
...
لن أَهرب للشمال
أَيّها الربّ
لا تحسبني من الذين يبحثون عن ملاذ.

ــــ سنكملُ لاحقاً هذا الحساب ــــ

عليَّ أَن أَمضي الآن إلى النوم:
لا أَريد أن أَتأخّر عن باص الكوابيس، الذاهبِ إلى صبرا وشاتيلا...

開往撒布拉和夏蒂拉的夢魔巴士

我看見他們把我的姨媽們裝進黑色的塑膠袋
她們溫熱的鮮血在塑膠袋的角落裏彙集
（可是我並沒有姨媽）
我知道他們殺害了娜塔莎——我三歲的小女兒
（可是我並沒有女兒）
我聽說他們強暴了我妻子，隨後把她的身體拖下樓梯，扔到大街上
（可是我並沒有結婚）
而這，一定是我那副被軍靴踩壞的眼鏡
（可是我並不戴眼鏡）
……
那時我正在父母家中安睡，夢中盼著去她家拜訪，可是當我醒來：
我看見我的兄弟姐妹
被掛在
復活教堂的天花板
連主都憐惜地歎道：「這是我的痛苦。」
而我則把所有懸掛者的尊嚴收好，回答：「不，這是我們的痛
　　苦！」
……
這痛苦灼灼發光，相比夢魘，更為我所喜愛。
……
我絕不會逃去北方
主啊
請你不要把我和那些逃難的人混為一談

——這個區別我們以後再談——

現在我該睡覺了
我不想錯過那班開往撒布拉和夏蒂拉的夢魘巴士

（牛子牧　譯）

譯註：
撒布拉、夏蒂拉為黎巴嫩貝魯特附近的巴勒斯坦難民聚集地。1982 年黎巴嫩內戰期間，黎巴嫩基督教民兵組織在兩地犯下大屠殺罪行，受害者多為巴勒斯坦人和黎巴嫩什葉派穆斯林。

The Nightmare Bus to Sabra and Shatila

I saw them stuff my aunts into black plastic bags
the warm blood pooling inside
(but I have no aunts)
I knew they killed Natasha, my three-year-old daughter
(but I have no daughter)
I was told they raped my wife
then dragged her body down the stairs
and left it in the street
(but I never married)
No doubt about it: those are my glasses
crushed beneath their boots
(but I don't wear glasses)
…
Asleep in my parents' house, I dreamt
of traveling to see her, and when I woke
I saw my brothers
hanging from the ceiling
of the Church of the Holy Sepulchre
The Lord in His mercy said, "This is my suffering"
and I, gathering up the dignity
of those who were hung
said, "No it's our own"
…
Now suffering's glow is dearer
even than my nightmares
…

Lord
I won't flee to the north—
don't count me among those seeking refuge

—We'll settle accounts later—

Time to sleep now
I don't want to miss
the nightmare bus to Sabra and Shatila

(Translated by Kareem James Abu-Zeid)

Translator's Note:
Sabra and Shatila were two camps for Palestinian refugees located in Beirut. During the Israeli invasion of Lebanon in 1982, a Lebanese Christian militia allied with Israel carried out a massacre of the camps' residents.

揚・米歇爾・埃斯比達列，生於1957 年，擅長各種樂器，不斷創新語言行為模式，挑戰語言的界限。他曾創辦《Java》雜誌，並在《文學》（*littéraire*）雜誌編輯「新法文詩歌」專號。曾出版數本書，包括非常具爭議性的《碎片：當代法文詩歌選》(2000) 和《工具箱：當代法文詩歌全景》(2006)。他的詩集《埃斯比達列理論》出版於2003 年，其英譯本出版於2005 年；《屠夫夢幻》出版於2001 年，其英譯本出版於2003 年。埃斯比達列從事各種多媒體創作，包括聲音、視頻、音樂等。他也曾任朋克搖滾樂隊的鼓手，並經常在法國及國外舉行詩歌朗誦會、講座和表演。

Jean-Michel Espitallier (born 1957) works along constantly renewed modes of action to create new vocabularies and test the limits of language. As co-founder of the journal *Java* and coordinator of the issue about "New French Poetry" in the magazine *littéraire* (March 2001), he is also the author of several books including the very controversial *Pièces detaches: une anthologie de la poésie française aujourd'hui* (2000) translated into English as *Bits and Pieces: An Anthology of French Poetry Today* (2000) and *Caisse à outils: un panorama de la poésie française aujourd'hui* (*Tool Box: A Panorama of French Poetry Today*, 2006). His *Le Théorème d'Espitallier* (2003) was translated into English by Guy Bennett (*Espitallier's Theorem*, 2005) while *Fantaisie bouchère* (2001) was translated by Sherry Brennan (*Butcher's Fantasy*, 2003). He works on various multimedia projects, is a drummer for a punk-rock band, and gives readings, performances and lectures in France and abroad.

揚・米歇爾・埃斯比達列

JEAN-MICHEL ESPITALLIER

Make war not war (comment j'ai raté la guerre)

« Je vois les yeux qui ont vu l'Empereur. »
Roland Barthes

Pellicules, indices, petits récits.
Toujours là et toujours absente.

... les films de René Vautier, la gare de l'Est, la *Jeanne-d'Arc* d'Heller, Otto Dix, le grondement des bombardiers américains survolant la France pendant la première guerre du Golfe, une peinture de Zeno Diemer représentant deux zeppelins accrochés par des projecteurs sur les côtes anglaises en 1915, les blindés Solido à chenillettes métal (AMX-13 bitubes, Tigre, Jagpanther), *Voyage au bout de l'enfer*, la « Sonnerie aux morts » dans le silence des 11 Novembre, Timisoara à la télévision, les impacts de balles sur la cathédrale de Dunkerque, les impacts de balles sur le Sacré-Cœur, les impacts de balles dans le no man's land de Nicosie, *Nord*, les véhicules militaires Dinky Toys, le portrait de Jean Moulin « à l'écharpe », les premiers témoignages du génocide des Khmers rouges, Ratko Mladic à la télévision, les soldats Airfix, le 11e BCA, *Lili Marlène*, les cris d'une femme, à la radio, après un attentat de l'OAS, la guerre du Liban à la télévision, « la guerre de 39—la guerre de 39–40—l'Occupation—la guerre—la guerre de 40—39-40—la dernière guerre », les *Feuillets d'Hypnos*, les anciens d'Indo, l'odeur du treillis, les promenades dominicales au fort de Roche-Lacroix, la tranchée des baïonnettes avec mes parents, *Tombeau pour 500 000 soldats*, les douilles d'obus en cuivre cintrées et ouvragées que ma grand-mère utilisait comme pots de fleurs, le drapeau tricolore, *Shoah*, *Les Sentiers de la gloire*, les wagons à bestiaux, *Tora ! Tora ! Tora !*, Christian Boltanski, la batterie antiaérienne sur le toit de mon hôtel à Bagdad, mon professeur d'histoire, déporté à Dachau, qui nous avait apporté sa tenue rayée, les gueules cassées, un fort Vauban au bord de la route, le brassard FFI de mon père, les images du Biafra dans *Paris-Match*, le procès Eichmann, la voisine de mes parents qui me faisait écouter de la musique militaire, le plateau du Vercors, « la guerre est la continuation de la politique par d'autres moyens », *La Grande Vadrouille*, les histoires de parachutages, l'hôtel Lutétia, les images du Vietnam dans *Woodstock* (« give me an F, give me a U... »), les impacts de balles sur les casernes désaffectées de La Condamine, le 8 mai devenu férié sous Giscard, le dépôt de gerbe au monument aux morts, les rangées de chars d'assaut rouillés dans la banlieue de Bagdad, un casque de poilu, *Le Pont de la rivière Kwaï*, le fort de Saint-Vincent-les-Forts où a été interné Jean Giono en 1944, le checkpoint à Nicosie, ma mère racontant qu'elle avait vu passer le wagon blindé de Göring à Bordighera, « Le Déserteur », le général de Gaulle en uniforme de général, *Apocalypse Now*, « La Guerre » en une de *Libération* lors du déclenchement de la guerre du Golfe, *Johnny got his gun*, les harkis dans des tentes, la 22 long rifle douze coups automatiques qu'un mercenaire, retour du Katanga, voulait vendre à mon père, Drancy, les petits portraits en médaillon des morts pour la France sur certaines tombes du cimetière, la visite du camp de Matthausen en Autriche, *La Question*, les guerres indiennes dans les westerns, « L'appel du 18 Juin » affiché dans ma salle de classe, les hélicoptères transports de troupe en forme de bananes, « Le Chant des partisans », mon tank Joustra, les plaques dans les rues de Paris à la mémoire des résistants tués à la Libération, l'Intifada à la télevision, l'Angola à la télévision, mon oncle Jean se souvenant des deux résistants pendus par les Allemands, place Masséna, à Nice, ma mère à vingt ans sur les chars des Américains (chewing-gum et Craven A), « Entre ici, Jean Moulin, avec ton terrible cortège », Goya, *Kapo*, la gare d'Arenc, l'ossuaire de Douaumont, les surplus militaires, l'entrée des troupes serbes dans Srebrenica en direct à la radio, *Les Hommes contre*, mon poster de Che Guevara, les GMC, des tickets de rationnement conservés par ma mère, *Sunday Bloody Sunday*, « Radio Paris ment/Radio Paris est allemand », la chute de Saigon et l'image des hélicoptères sur le toit de l'ambassade US, la forêt de Rethondes avec mes parents, *La Bataille du rail*, le Rwanda à la télévision, les blockhaus italiens sur la route de Cuneo, les topinambours et les rutabagas, « Fabrice à Waterloo », les avions Starfix (Lightning, Mig 21, Stuka, Hawker Typhoon, Dornier), Georges Béraud défiguré par une grenade, Léopold Occelli au STO en Allemagne, le cousin Félix tué devant Stuttgart à la fin du mois d'avril 1945, Marie Ponza blessée par balle alors qu'elle ravitaillait les maquis, Léo Michel racontant la prise de Monte Cassino avec les Goums, la guerre des Malouines à la télévision et la fin du *Sheffield* frappé par un Exocet en une de *Libération*, les Forces françaises en Allemagne, le fil de fer barbelé, *Refus d'obéissance*, Sarajevo et le retour du mot *snipers*, le Vietnam (napalm, Rauschenberg, défoliants), avoir été le contemporain de Franco, *Un pont trop loin*, les rumeurs sur les anciens collaborateurs, *La 317e section*, quelques cartes postales de « villages détruits » de la Première Guerre mondiale, le jeu du Risk, les alignements de croix blanches des cimetières américains en Normandie, *La Destruction des Juifs d'Europe* de Raul Hilberg, Loulou Boisramé tué à côté de mon père lors de la libération de Gap, les images du bombardement du marché de Sarajevo, « War. Comprehensive coverage » (*Los Angeles Times*, avril 2003), le brouillage des messages personnels dans les films sur l'Occupation, les témoignages de Sabra et Chatila, tante Hélène à qui l'on donna un bureau de tabac en tant que veuve de guerre, les Scud sur Israël à la télévision, la Maison du poilu, *Sandinista*, les boat people, la petite croix de Lorraine que portait ma mère à l'intérieur de son veston pendant l'Occupation, un voisin devenu sourd parce qu'il avait été artilleur en Indochine, *La Débâcle*, « l'équilibre de la terreur », la Tchétchénie à la télévision, « Les sanglots longs des violons de l'automne », le casque bleu « UN » de Jo, retour du Liban, les soldats Starlux, la plaque apposée sur un mur de mon lycée à la mémoire de plusieurs résistants fusillés, le débarquement américain en Somalie en direct à la télévision, l'oreille de mon père entaillée par une balle allemande, « War is over », *Orages d'acier*, les appelés d'Algérie, le MAS-36 transformé de mon père, *Nuit et brouillard*, Ground Zero...

Pellicules, indices, petits récits.

Jamais pas là jamais là.

要戰爭，不要戰爭
(我是怎樣錯過了戰爭)

「我看到一雙曾經見過拿破崙皇帝的眼睛。」
——羅蘭·巴特

膠片，線索，小故事
始終在場卻永遠缺席。

……勒內·弗提耶的電影，巴黎東站，Heller的聖女貞德號戰艦，奧托迪·克斯，第一次海灣戰爭時美軍轟炸的隆隆聲響徹法國上空，澤諾·迪耶美的一副油畫，畫上是1915年的英國海岸，探照燈下的兩艘齊泊林飛艇並肩飛行，鐵鍊的Solido坦克(AMX-13雙炮管坦克、虎式坦克、獵豹式坦克)，電影《獵鹿人》，11月11日紀念戰爭犧牲者時，一片寂靜中響起的法國軍號，蒂米什瓦拉上了電視，敦克爾克大教堂和巴黎聖心殿的彈痕，無人之境尼古西亞的彈痕，《北方》，玩具軍車，讓·穆蘭戴著圍巾和禮帽的頭像，赤棉大屠殺的早期罪證，拉特科·姆拉迪奇上電視，塑膠模型士兵，法國阿爾卑斯山地作戰部隊第11營，《莉莉·馬蓮》，秘密軍隊組織的襲擊後一個女人在電臺裏的喊叫聲，電視上黎巴嫩戰爭的畫面，「1939年的戰爭，1939至1940年的戰爭，佔領時期，戰爭，1940年的戰爭，1939至1940年的戰爭，最後的戰爭」，《伊普諾斯的書頁》，越南的法國老兵，粗麻布的氣味，星期天和我的父母在羅什—拉克拉堡壘散步，刺刀戰壕，《50萬士兵的墳墓》，流線型的銅炮彈殼，我的祖母用它們來種花，三色旗，《納粹大屠殺》，電影《光榮之路》，運送牲畜的火車，日本片《虎虎虎》，克利斯蒂安·波爾坦斯基，地對空排炮飛躍我在巴格達的旅店，我的歷史老師，達濠集中營的倖存者，給我們看他的條形囚服，老兵的壞馬克杯，路旁的沃邦軍事堡壘，我父親的FFI(法國內部抵抗力量)的三色臂章，巴黎《競賽畫報》上比亞法拉共和國的畫面，埃希曼受審判，兒時給我聽軍樂的鄰居，維爾科爾高地，「戰爭是政治的繼續，只是方式不同。」，法國電影《虎口脱險》空降兵的場面，魯特西亞酒店，伍德斯托克中越南的畫面(「give me an F，give me a U...」)，孔達米訥廢棄營房上的彈痕，季斯卡總統時代五月8日成為假日，在紀念死者的建築前放花，一排排生銹的坦克橫在巴格達的郊外，一頂老式法軍頭盔，《桂河大橋》，1944年關押讓·吉亞諾的聖萬森雷弗堡壘，尼古西亞的哨站，我母親説她曾經在波爾蒂蓋拉親眼看見戈林封閉的火車車廂，反戰歌曲〈逃兵〉，身著戎裝的戴高樂將軍,《現代啟示錄》，海灣戰爭爆發時「戰爭」二字成為《自由報》的頭條，電影《無語問蒼天》，帳篷下阿爾及利亞的法國軍人，一個從剛果加丹加回來的外國兵，想把他的一把22寸口徑12發自動來福槍賣給我的父親，德朗西公墓，墓碑上烈士們的圓形頭像章，參觀奧地利毛特豪森集中營，《問題》，美國西部的印第安戰爭，我的教室裏貼著戴高樂〈六月18日的召喚〉，運送軍隊的直升機組成彎月的形狀,〈擁護者之歌〉，我的玩具坦克，為紀念法國解放運動中的被殺者，在巴黎街頭的紀念牌，巴以衝突中的反對派上了電視，安哥拉上了電視，我的叔叔讓記得，兩個抵抗運動者被德國人吊死在尼斯的馬塞納廣場，我母親二十歲時爬上了美國人的坦克(口香糖和克萊文A牌香煙)，「進來吧，讓·穆蘭，還有你厲害的同伴們。」高亞，《卡波》，阿蘭可火車站，杜奧蒙骸骨堆，軍裝，廣播直播塞爾維亞軍隊進入斯雷佈雷尼察，電影《寸土必爭》，我的切格瓦拉海報，GMC卡車，我母親保留的戰時配給票，《血紅的星期天》，

「巴黎的廣播在説謊/ 巴黎的廣播是德國人的」，西貢淪陷，美國大使館屋頂上的直升機，和我父母在雷通代森林，《鐵軌之戰》，盧旺達上了電視，庫內奧路旁的義大利碉堡，鬼子姜和甘藍，「布里斯在滑鐵盧」，Starfix 飛機 (Lightning，Mig 21，Stuka，Hawker Typhoon，Dornier)，被手榴彈破了相的喬治．貝戶，萊奧坡德．歐塞利在德國被強制勞動，1945 年四月底，表兄菲利克斯在斯圖加特被殺，瑪麗．彭匝給遊擊隊送食物的時候中槍負傷，萊歐．蜜雪兒講述和摩洛哥士兵的卡西諾戰役，馬島戰爭上了電視，謝菲爾德被飛魚反艦導彈打擊的畫面上了《自由報》頭條，法國軍隊在德國，鐵絲網,《拒絕服從》，塞拉耶佛和「狙擊手」這個詞的再次出現，越南(凝固汽油彈，羅斯申伯格，橙劑) 曾經是法國的現代藝術，電影《奪橋遺恨》，關於與德國合作者的種種謠言，電影《第317 分部》，幾張一戰〈摧毀的村莊〉明信片，戰爭軍棋，諾曼第美軍公墓一排排整齊的十字架，勞爾．希爾伯格寫的《歐洲猶太人的毀滅》，解放嘉普時，露露．博阿斯拉米在我父親身邊被殺，塞拉耶佛市場區被轟炸的畫面，〈戰爭保險賠償金〉(《洛杉磯時報》，2003 年四月)，在關於德國佔領法國的那些電影中，個人表達的干擾，薩布拉和莎緹拉的證言，大家把煙鋪給了艾蓮娜嬸嬸，因為她是戰爭寡婦，以色列飛毛腿導彈上了電視，la Maison du poilu，《桑地諾民族解放陣線》，越南船民，法國被佔領時期，我母親在衣服內裏佩戴的抵抗運動洛林十字，一個鄰居從越南當炮兵回來，耳朵聾了，左拉的《崩潰》,「冷戰的恐怖均勢」，車臣共和國上了電視，「秋天的小提琴悠長的嗚咽聲」，從黎巴嫩回來的Jo，有一頂聯合國維和部隊藍色頭盔，玩具士兵，我的高中校園牆上，有一塊紀念被槍殺的抵抗者的牌子，美國軍隊進入索馬里的畫面在電視上直播，我父親的一隻耳朵被德國人的子彈削去了一塊，「戰爭結束了」，《鋼暴雨》，阿爾及利亞的入伍青年，我父親改裝過的MAS-36 阿爾步槍，《夜與霧》，Ground Zero……

膠片，線索，小故事

永遠不在，不在。

(黃瑩雪　譯)

Make war not war (how I missed war)

"I see the eyes that have seen the Emperor."
Roland Barthes

Celluloid, clues, little stories.
Always there and always absent.
...the films of Rene Vautier, the East Station, the Heller *Jeanne d'Arc,* Otto Dix, the rumbling of American bombers flying over France during the first Gulf war, a painting by Zeno Diemer representing two zeppelins caught by spotlights on the English coast in 1915, the armored Solidos on metal tracks (AMX-13 Bi-Tubes, Tiger, Jagpanther), *The Deer Hunter*, the song "Aux morts" in the silence every November 11, Timisoara on television, the bullet holes in Dunkirk Cathedral, the bullet holes on Sacré-Cœur, the bullet holes in the Nicosia no-man's-land, *North*, Dinky Toy military vehicles, the portrait of Jean Moulin in "official dress," the first eyewitnesses of the genocides by the Khmer Rouge, Ratko Mladic on television, Airfix soldiers, the 11th BCA, *Lily Marlene*, the screams of a woman, on the radio, after an assassination attempt by the OAS, the Lebanese war on television, "the war of 39—the war of 39–40—the Occupation—the war—the war of 40—39–40—the last war," *Leaves of Hypnos*, the veterans of Indo, the smell of canvas uniforms, the Sunday walks to Fort Roche-Lacroix, the trenches of bayonets with my parents, *Tomb for 500,000 Soldiers*, the crazily dented copper cartridge casings my grandmother used as flower pots, the tricolor flag, *Shoah*, *Paths of Glory*, the cattle cars, *Tora! Tora! Tora!*, Christian Boltanski, the anti-aerial battery on the roof of my hotel in Baghdad, my history teacher, deported to Dachau, who brought us his striped outfit, the broken mugs of vets, a Vauban Fort on the side of the road, my father's FFI armband, the images of Biafra in *Paris-Match*, the Eichmann trial, my parents' neighbor who made me listen to her military music, the Vercors Plateau, "war is nothing more than the continuation of politics by other means," *The Big Runaround*, the stories of paratrooper drops, the Lutetia Hotel, the images of Vietnam at *Woodstock* ("give me an F, give me a U ..."), the bullet holes on the abandoned barracks of La Condamine, May 8 made a holiday by Giscard, the laying of wreaths on war memorials, the rows of assault tanks rusting in the suburbs of Baghdad, a veteran's helmet, *The Bridge on the River Kwai*, Fort Saint-Vincent-les-Forts where Jean Giono was interned in 1944, the checkpoint at Nicosia, my mother telling how she saw Goring's armored car pass in Bordighera, "The Deserter," General de Gaulle in the uniform of a general, *Apocalypse Now*, "War" on the front of *Liberation* at the launch of the Gulf war, *Johnny Got His Gun*, the Harkis in tents, the 12 gauge .22 automatic long rifle that a mercenary, returned from Katanga, wanted to sell to my father, Drancy, the little medallion portraits of those who died for France on some of the graves in the cemetery, the visit to Camp Matthausen in Austria, *La Question*, Indian battles in westerns, "The Appeal of June 18" posted in my classroom, troop transport choppers in the shape of bananas, the "Chant des Partisans," my Joustra tank, the plaques on Parisian streets in memory of resistance fighters killed in the Liberation, the Intifada on television, Angola on television, my uncle Jean remembering two resistance fighters hung by

the Germans, Place Massena, in Nice, my mother at 20 on the tanks of the Americans (chewing gum and Craven A), "Enter now, Jean Moulin, with your terrible cortege," Goya, *Kapo*, the Arenc station, the Douaumont ossuary, military surplus, the entry of Serbian troops into Srebrenica live on the radio, *Many Wars Ago*, my poster of Che Guevara, the GMC, some ration coupons my mother saved, *Sunday Bloody Sunday*, "Radio Paris lies / Radio Paris is German," the fall of Saigon and the image of helicopters on the roof of the U.S. Embassy, the Rethondes forest with my parents, *The Battle of the Rails*, Rwanda on television, the Italian blockhaus on the Cuneo road, Jerusalem artichokes and rutabagas, "Fabrice in Waterloo," the Starfix airplanes (Lightning, Mig 21, Stuka, Hawker Typhoon, Dornier), George Beraud disfigured by a grenade, Leopold Occelli in the STO in Germany, my cousin Felix killed before Stuttgart at the end of the month of April 1945, Marie Ponza wounded by a bullet as she brought supplies to the maquis, Leo Michel recounting the capture of Monte Cassino with the Goums, the Falkland war on television and the end of *Sheffield* hit by an Exocet on the front page of *Liberation*, the French forces in Germany, barbed wire, *Refusal to Obey*, Sarajevo and the return of the word "snipers," Vietnam (napalm, Rauschenberg, defoliant), having been the contemporary of Franco, *A Bridge Too Far*, the rumors about old collaborators, *The 317th Platoon*, some postcards of "destroyed villages" of the First World War, the game of Risk, the lines of white crosses in the American cemeteries in Normandy, Raul Hilberg's *The Destruction of the European Jews*, Loulou Boisrame killed beside my father during the liberation of Gap, the images of the bombing of the market in Sarajevo, "War. Comprehensive coverage" (*Los Angeles Times*, April 2003), the jamming of personal communications in films about the Occupation, the eyewitnesses from Sabra and Chatila, aunt Helene who was given a *tabac* as a war widow, the Scuds over Israel on television, the Poilu Lodge, *Sandinista*, the boat people, the little cross of Lorraine that my mother carried inside her jacket during the Occupation, a neighbor deafened by being an artilleryman in Indochina, *The Debacle*, "equilibrium-through-terror," Chechnya on television, "Les sanglots longs des violons de l'automne," Jo's U.N. blue beret, return from Lebanon, Starlux soldiers, the plaque affixed to a wall in my high school to the memory of several resistance fighters shot, the American invasion of Somalia live on television, my father's ear nicked by a German bullet, "War is over," *Storm of Steel*, Algerian conscripts, my father's modified MAS-36, *Night and Fog*, Ground Zero...

Celluloid, clues, little stories.

Never not there never there.

(Translated by Pascale-Anne Brault and Sherry Brennan)

justification

L'axe du bien

Nous sommes l'axe du bien. Nous faisons le bien et portons le bien au mal qui fait du mal au bien. Nous sommes l'axe du bien. Nous sommes l'axe du bien en lutte contre le mal. Contre l'axe du mal. L'axe du mal fait le mal où se trouve le bien. Nous sommes l'axe du bien en lutte contre le mal. L'axe du mal fait le mal au bien qui lutte contre le mal. Nous sommes les forces du bien pour le bien des forces du bien qui luttent afin de rétablir le bien de l'axe du mal. Nous sommes les forces du bien. Le mal de l'axe du mal fait mal au bien qui est le bien et nous devons lutter contre leur bien qui est le mal. Ils sont l'axe du mal. Nous sommes l'axe du bien. L'axe du mal porte le mal au bien qui est son mal. L'axe du bien porte le bien au mal qui est son mal. L'axe du bien porte le bien au bien du mal qui est son mal. Nous sommes les forces du bien et nous devons faire mal au mal pour le bien de l'axe du mal dont le bien est le mal. Nous sommes l'axe du bien. Ils sont l'axe du mal. Le bien voit que le mal est mal parce qu'il est le bien. Seul l'axe du mal fait le mal et veut du mal au bien ou ne veut pas de bien à ce qu'il pense être le mal et qui est le bien. Nous sommes le forces du bien en lutte contre les forces du mal qui veulent notre mal. Nous faisons mal aux forces de l'axe du mal pour notre bien car leur bien est notre mal et le bien est le mal que nous faisons à leur bien qui fait le mal au bien. Le bien triomphera des forces du mal. Le bien fera triompher le bien. Le bien fera triompher le bien des forces du bien. Le bien ne peut faire triompher le bien que parce qu'il est le bien. Nous sommes les forces du bien et nous devons faire mal à l'axe du mal. Au nom du bien. Contre le bien des forces du mal. Au nom du bien des forces du bien en lutte contre les forces du mal. Nous sommes les forces du bien. Ils sont les forces du mal. Nous sommes le bien et nous voulons du mal aux forces du mal qui nous veulent du mal. Nous sommes les forces du bien et nous voulons du mal aux forces du mal pour leur bien. Non sans mal. Le bien du mal est le mal. Le bien du bien est le bien. Le bien du bien est le mal pour le mal. Le mal du bien est encore le bien. Le bien de l'axe du mal est toujours le mal. Ils veulent du mal à notre bien qu'ils jugent être le mal et qui est le bien. Non sans mal. Nous sommes l'axe du bien. Nous voudrons du bien à l'axe du mal quand il sera devenu l'axe du bien. Non sans mal. Les forces du bien reconnaissent l'axe du mal à ce qu'il est le mal. Les forces du bien reconnaissent le mal à ce qu'il n'est pas le bien. Les forces du bien reconnaissent le mal à ce que l'axe du bien lui veut du mal. Les forces du bien sont le bien parce qu'en tant que forces du bien elles ne peuvent qu'incarner le bien. Non sans mal. L'axe du bien est le bien parce que l'axe du mal lui veut du mal. L'axe du bien fera triompher le bien des forces du mal parce qu'elles sont le mal et qu'il est le bien. Non sans mal.

février/mars 2003

辯解

正義的代表

我們是正義的代表。我們行善，因此讓邪惡得到發展，因而傷害了善。我們是正義的代表。 我們是正義的代表，與邪惡鬥爭。對抗邪惡的一方。邪惡勢力傷害正義的所在。我們是正義的代表，與惡鬥爭。邪惡勢力傷害正義，而正是正義在對抗邪惡。我們是正義的力量，為了正義力量能壯大而鬥爭，也為了邪惡勢力能轉好。 我們是正義的力量。邪惡勢力的罪惡傷害正義並發展膨脹，我們應該和這種發展進行鬥爭，因為這是邪惡的。他們是邪惡的代表。我們是正義的代表。邪惡的一方將惡帶給善，這是善所不喜歡的。正義的一方將善帶給惡，這也是惡所不喜歡的。正義的一方將善帶給惡中之善，這是他所不喜歡的。我們是正義的力量，我們應該為了邪惡勢力著想，去摧毀他們，因為他們的發展是邪惡的。我們是正義的代表。他們是邪惡的代表。正義能看清邪惡，因為他自身是正義的。只有邪惡勢力會對他認定為邪惡的物件進行破害，詛咒或不懷好意，而他們認定的對象就是正義。我們是正義的力量，與對我們不懷好意的邪惡力量鬥爭。為了我們的發展，我們損害邪惡勢力的力量，因為他們的發展將是我們的不幸，而其中之大幸就是我們對他們造成的傷害，因為他們是邪惡的。善面對惡必將大獲全勝。善定會讓正義發揚光大。善定會讓正義的力量發揚光大。善必定毫無疑問會大獲全勝，因為善是正義的。我們是正義的力量，我們必須要破害邪惡勢力。以正義的名義。反對邪惡力量的發展。為了正義力量的壯大，與邪惡力量鬥爭。我們是正義的力量，而他們是邪惡的力量。我們是善，我們要破害邪惡的力量，因為他們想要傷害我們。我們是正義的力量，我們破害邪惡力量，都是為了他們好。沒有惡意。邪惡的膨脹是壞的。正義的壯大是好的。正義的發展，就是邪惡的敗壞。而正義的不幸，仍然是正義的。邪惡勢力的發展，必然還是邪惡的。他們想傷害我們的正義，因為他們恰恰認為我們的正義是邪惡的。沒有惡意。我們是正義的代表。等到邪惡勢力轉變為正義時，我們會對他充滿好意。沒有惡意。正義的力量能辨認出邪惡勢力中的惡。正義的力量能辨認出誰是惡，誰不是善。正義的力量能辨認出正義的一方想要破害的邪惡勢力。正義的力量是善的，因為身為正義力量，他只能代表善良和正義。 沒有惡意。正義的一方是善的，因為邪惡勢力想要傷害他。正義的代表定會大敗邪惡勢力，讓正義發揚光大，因為對手是惡，而自己是善。沒有惡意。

2003 年2 月至3 月

(黃瑩雪　譯)

Justification
The Axis of Good

We are the axis of good. We do good and bring good to the evil who do evil to the good. We are the axis of good. We are the axis of good in the fight against evil. Against the axis of evil. The axis of evil does evil where good is found. We are the axis of good in the fight against evil. The axis of evil does evil to the good who fight against evil. We are the forces of good for the good of the forces of good who fight in the end to restore the good of the axis of evil. We are the forces of good. The evil of the axis of evil do evil to the good who are good and we must fight against their good which is evil. They are the axis of evil. We are the axis of good. The axis of evil brings evil to the good who are its evil. The axis of good brings good to the evil who are its evil. The axis of good brings good for the good of the evil who are its evil. We are the forces of good and we must do evil to evil for the good of the axis of evil whose good is evil. We are the axis of good. They are the axis of evil. The good sees that the evil is evil because it is good. Only the axis of evil does evil and wishes evil on the good or does not wish good to what it thinks to be evil and which is good. We are the forces of good in the fight against the forces of evil who wish us evil. We do evil to the forces of the axis of evil for our good because their good is our evil and the good is evil that we do for the good of those who do evil to the good. The good will triumph over the forces of evil. The good will make good triumph. The good will make the good of the forces of good triumph. The good can make good triumph only because it is good. We are the forces of good and we must do evil to the axis of evil. In the name of good. Against the good of the forces of evil. In the name of the good of the forces of good in the fight against the forces of evil. We are the forces of good. They are the forces of evil. We are good and we wish evil to the forces of evil who wish us evil. We are the forces of good and we wish evil to the forces of evil for their good. Though we are bedeviled. The good of the evil is evil. The good of the good is good. The good of the good is evil for the evil. The evil of the good is still good. The good of the axis of evil is always evil. They wish evil to our good which they judge to be evil and which is good. Though we are bedeviled. We are the axis of good. We will wish good to the axis of evil when it has become the axis of good. Though we are bedeviled. The forces of good recognize the axis of evil in that it is evil. The forces of good recognize the evil in that it is not good. The forces of good recognize the evil in that the axis of good wishes it evil. The forces of good are the good insofar as the forces of good can incarnate only good. Though we are bedeviled. The axis of good is the good because the axis of evil wishes it evil. The axis of good will make good triumph over the forces of evil because they are evil and it is the good. Though we are bedeviled.

February/March 2003

(Translated by Pascale-Anne Brault and Sherry Brennan)

詹瑪・歌爾伽，1968年出生於巴塞隆納，在巴塞隆納大學取得文獻學博士學位，現於該校任教古典文學課程。歌爾伽出版過六本詩集，包括《鳥類學》(1997)、《手的障礙》(2003)、《光學儀器》(2005)、《書頁時刻》(2006)、《隔膜》(2013)和《牆》(2015)，另有合著非虛構類書籍《自然廚房裏：飯桌上的健康、傳統與快樂》(2004)。歌爾伽在印度新德里梵文基金會任駐留詩人三個月後，陸續在翻譯印度當代英文詩歌，現已出版狄麗普・切特熱的詩集《邁向死亡的二十次早餐》(2013)。歌爾伽詩作的英譯被收錄於《加泰隆尼亞詩人六家》(弧形出版社，2013)。

Gemma Gorga, born in Barcelona in 1968, has a Ph.D. in Philology from the University of Barcelona, where she works as a teacher of Ancient Literature. She has published six collections of poetry: *Ocellania* (*Birdology*, 1997), *El desordre de les mans* (*Disorder of the Hands*, 2003), *Instruments òptics* (*Optical Instruments*, 2005), *Llibre dels minuts* (*Book of Minutes*, 2006), *Diafragma* (*Diaphragm*, 2013, with the photographer Joan Ramell) and *Mur* (*Wall*, 2015). Among her non-fiction works, she has published *Within the Natural Kitchen: Health, Tradition and Pleasure at the Table* (2004, with Antonio Lozano). Following a three-month residence with the Sanskriti Foundation in New Delhi, she translated the work of contemporary anglophone Indian poet Dilip Chitre *Vint esmorzars cap a la mort* (*Twenty Breakfasts Towards Death*, 2013). A selection of Gorga's poems has been included in Pere Ballart's anthology *Six Catalan Poets*, published by Arc Publications in 2013.

詹瑪・歌爾伽

GEMMA GORGA

Pedres

Si la veu pogués sortir a les fotografies
com hi surt l'ombra o la tendresa—tot i ser
realitats més vulnerables—, sentiria
un cop més el meu pare explicant-me que, abans
de collir una pedra, cal fer-la rodolar
amb el peu o amb una branca per espantar
els escorpins que s'hi amaguen com punxes seques.
Mai no vaig preocupar-me'n. Perquè tenir sis
anys era senzill, senzill com morir-se. En tots
dos casos, no hi havia més secret que l'aire:
respirar-lo o no respirar-lo, com si l'ànima
fos plena de diminuts alvèols que s'obren
i es tanquen. El primer escorpí que vaig veure
va ser al llibre de ciències naturals,
atrapat per sempre entre les pinces severes
del temps. De vegades, però, els llibres no expliquen
tota la veritat, com si no la sabessin
o l'haguessin oblidat camí de la impremta.
Aràcnid que té el cos dividit en abdomen
i cefalotòrax. Res no hi deia del sol
ardent a la llengua, de la por, de l'espiga
travessada al coll. Jo no sabia llavors
que les paraules són immensos icebergs
que oculten sota les aigües glaçades molt
més del que mostren. Com la paraula *escorpí*.
I ara, mentre el telèfon sona insistentment
—un crit agut de matinada—, mentre em llevo,
encenc el llum, acosto la mà al seu cos blanc
de plàstic que brilla com una pedra al sol,
mentre el despenjo, i dic *sí?*, i algú em diu que ets mort,
jo només penso en els escorpins, en allò
que volies dir-me quan repeties *fes*
rodar les pedres, sisplau, fes rodar les pedres.

石

如果聲音能夠在照片上出現
像陰影或觸痛般出現——儘管
它們是更脆弱的現實——我再聽到
我父親告訴我，撿
一塊石頭前，必須讓它挑開，
使用腳或樹枝讓它挑開
趕走藏在石底如乾荊棘般的蠍子。
我從沒擔心過。六歲時
生和死一樣容易。這兩件事，
除了空氣甚麼秘密都沒有：
呼吸或不呼吸，彷彿靈魂
充滿微小的肺泡，它們在開放
和閉合。我第一次見到蠍子
就是在自然科學課本裏，
牠被時間的重鐳永遠地
抓住。雖然，有時候，書真話不
全説，就像它們不知道
或者在去印廠路上，它們把真話忘了。
「蠍子的身體分為腹部
和頭胸部。」關於舌頭上火辣辣
的太陽，害怕，尖鋒扎進脖子
課本都沒有提到。當時我不知道
説是巨大的冰山
隱藏在冰冷水域下的
總比表現出來的更多。像「蠍子」字似的。
而現在，當我手機執拗地響起
（一陣尖鋭的叫聲），我起床，
開燈，伸手取白色塑料蓋手機
它就像在陽光下閃耀的石頭
我接電話説「喂？」就聽到有人説你死了，
我只想起蠍子，我多想
你對我説這句話：
「把石頭挑開，當心，把石頭挑開。」

(Jesús Sayols　譯)

Stones

If the voice could come out in photographs
in the way shadow or tenderness does—even while
being more vulnerable realities—I would hear
once again my father telling me that, before
picking up a stone, you should roll it over
with your foot or a branch to scare away
the scorpions hiding underneath like dry thorns.
I never worried about that. Being six years old
was simple, simple as dying. In both cases,
there was no secret other than the air:
breathing it or not breathing it, as if the soul
were full of tiny alveoli that open
and close. The first scorpion I saw
was in the natural science book,
trapped forever in the severe pincers
of time. On occasion, though, books don't tell
the whole truth, as if they didn't know it
or had forgotten it on the way from the printer's.
Arachnid with body divided into abdomen
and cephalothorax. It said nothing of the burning
sun in the tongue, of fear, of the spike
pierced into the neck. I didn't know then
that words are immense icebergs
hiding beneath their icy waters much
more than they show. Like the word *scorpion*.
And now, as the phone insistently rings
—a sharp daybreak cry—as I get up,
turn on the light, move my hand to its white body
of plastic that shines like a stone in the sun,
as I pick it up and say *yes?* and someone tells me you're dead,
I only think of scorpions, of what
you wanted to tell me when you repeated *roll*
the stones over, please, roll the stones over.

(Translated by Julie Wark)

Semàntica i nutrició

Cau la fulla a terra i es descompon
en significats menors—humitat,
pigment, làmina, oxigen, escalfor,
llum—, com qui lletreja el seu nom sencer
a un desconegut: *an hí drid car bò nic*.
Res no es perd pel camí, ni les converses
que ha mantingut amb la pluja de nit,
ni les lliçons de vol que li han donat
els ocells: tota ella es descompon
en unitats menors directament
assimilables per la paciència
de les formigues, les boques callades
del bosc. És per això que l'idioma
del vent arriba a parlar-se també
sota terra. I és per això que els cucs
s'emproven ales i surten volant
convertits en papallones. Tot és
matèria. Tot es transforma en vol
quan una simple fulla cau a terra.

語義和營養

葉子落在地上，就分解成
微笑的含義——濕，
顏，片，氧，熱，
光——，像對一個陌生人拼出
它全名：二、氧、化、碳。
路上沒丟失甚麼，包括它
和夜雨的談話，
鳥的飛
行課：全分解成
小小的細項，通過
螞蟻的耐心
直接同化，就像沉默的嘴
在森林裏。這就是為甚麼
風的語言來去
能在地下言說。這就是為甚麼
蚯蚓試試翅，就飛起來
好像蝴蝶一樣。一切都是
物質。一切都飛起來
當一片葉子落在地上。

(Jesús Sayols　譯)

Semantics and Nutrition

A leaf falls to the ground and decomposes
into smaller meanings—humidity,
pigment, lamina, oxygen, warmth,
light—, like someone spelling his full name
to a stranger: *car bon di o xi de*.
Nothing is lost on the way, neither
the talks with the rain at night,
nor the flight lessons given
by birds: it decomposes in its entirety
into smaller units directly assimilable
through the patience of ants, the silent mouths
of the forest. This is why the language
of the wind comes also to be spoken
underground. And this is why worms
try on wings and fly away
transformed into butterflies. Everything is
matter. Everything takes flight
when a single leaf falls to the ground.

(Translated by Anna Crowe)

Petit conte

L'abella se m'acostà als llavis per dictar-me
l'inici d'un poema trobat a l'atzar
entre les síl·labes dolces del taronger.
Hauria estat senzill tancar els ulls i assentir
si no fos perquè ningú no em va ensenyar mai
a acceptar un miracle. Sé perfectament
com s'han de posar les mans per rebre una poma
enverinada, sé com s'ha d'inclinar el coll
per sentir la lenta mossegada vermella
de la nit, com s'acumula la crueltat
al fons de tots els miralls. Quines són les mans,
però, amb què es pren una ofrena? Com cal obrir-les
per acceptar el do inesperat? L'endemà
sempre és massa tard: l'abella no hi és, no queden
flors en cap taronger, i les síl·labes no troben
l'ordre adequat per indicar el final feliç.

小故事

蜜蜂飛近我嘴唇，口述
一首詩的第一行
在橙樹的甜美音節中被偶然找到。
我好容易閉上了眼睛，同意了
但是沒有人教給我
怎樣接受一個奇蹟。我深知
怎樣用手接受一個
毒蘋果，怎樣彎曲脖子
去感覺黑夜慢慢地
深紅地咬下去，也知道殘忍怎麼堆積
在每一塊鏡子的底面。不過，該用哪一隻手
接受祭品？如何打開手
接受意外的禮物？後天
總是太晚：蜜蜂不在，橙樹花
不見，音節尋不著
適當的秩序來揭開幸福的結局。

(Jesús Sayols 譯)

Little Story

The bee came close to my lips to dictate to me
the beginning of a poem found by chance
among the sweet syllables of the orange tree.
It would have been simple to shut my eyes and agree
if it weren't that nobody ever showed me
how to accept a miracle. I know perfectly well
how to place my hands to receive a poisoned
apple, I know how to bend my neck
to feel the slow crimson bite
night makes, how cruelty accumulates
in the depths of every mirror. With what hands,
however, should a gift be taken? How to open the hands
to accept the unexpected gift? The following day
it is always too late: the bee has vanished, no flowers
remain on any orange tree, and the syllables can't find
the proper order to show what the happy ending might be.

(Translated by Anna Crowe)

Postguerra

El venerable Agató va viure tres anys
amb una pedra a la boca
per tal d'aprendre a guardar silenci.

L'àvia no va haver de viure tres anys
amb una pedra a la boca
per tal d'aprendre a guardar silenci.

戰後

古老聖阿伽頌在嘴裏含了三年[1]
時間的一塊石頭
是用來學習怎麼保持緘默的。

老奶奶在嘴裏含了三年
時間的一塊石頭
並不是用來學習怎麼保持緘默的。

(Jesús Sayols　譯)

Postwar

The venerable Agathon lived for three years
with a stone in his mouth
in order to learn to keep quiet.

My grandmother did not have to live for three years
with a stone in her mouth
in order to learn to keep quiet.

(Translated by Anna Crowe)

譯註：
1. 詩中的「三年」，即1936至1939年的西班牙內戰。

金惠順，生於南韓，在建國大學取得韓國文學博士學位。她從1979 年就開始發表詩歌，在雜誌《文學與文智》上發表了〈詩人抽煙〉等五首詩，此後她出版了十本詩集，包括《來自別的恆星》(1981)、《父親的稻草人》(1984)、《某恆星的地獄》(1987)、《我們的負片照》(1991)、《首爾，我的奧義書》(1994)、《可憐的愛情機器》(1997)、《給日曆工廠經理》(2000)、《一杯紅玻璃》(2004)、《你的第一次》(2008)、《憂鬱牙膏和玻璃鏡奶油》(2011) 等。她的詩也被翻譯成英文出版：《媽媽肯定是一個羽毛噴泉》(2008) 和《全世界的垃圾，聯合起來！》(2011)。她贏得的獎項包括「金洙暎文學獎」(1997)、「素月詩文學獎」(2000)、「未堂文學獎」(2006) 等。金惠順現居首爾，於首爾藝術大學教授創意寫作。

Kim Hyesoon was born in South Korea. She received her Ph.D. in Korean Literature from Konkuk University. Beginning as a poet in 1979 with the publication of "Poet Smoking a Cigarrette" and four other poems in *Literature and Intellect*, she has published ten poetry collections including: *From Another Star* (1981), *My Father's Scarecrow* (1984), *The Hell of a Certain Star* (1987), *The Negative of Our Image* (1991), *My Upanishad, Seoul* (1994), *Poor Love Machine* (1997), *To the Calendar Factory Manager* (2000), *A Glass of Red Mirror* (2004), *Your First* (2008), and *Sorrowtoothpaste Mirrorcream* (2011). Her poetry collections have been translated into English, including *Mommy Must be a Fountain of Feathers* (2008), and *All the Garbage of the World, Unite!* (2011). She has received numerous literary prizes including the Kim Su-yong Literary Award (1997), the Sowol Poetry Literature Award (2000) and the Midang Literature Award (2006). She lives in Seoul and teaches creative writing at the Seoul Institute of Arts.

金惠順

KIM HYESOON

내 안의 소금 원피스

슬픔을 참으면 몸에서 소금이 난다
짜디짠 당신의 표정
일평생 바다의 격렬한 타격에 강타당한 외로운 섬
같은 짐승의 눈빛

짧은 속눈썹 울타리 사이
파랑주의보 높아 바닷물 들이치는 날도 있었지만
소금의 건축이 허물어지지는 않았다
따가운 흐느낌처럼 손끝에서 피던 소금꽃

소금, 내 고꾸라진 그림자를 가루내어 가로등 아래 뿌렸다
소금, 내 몸속에서 유전하는 바다의 건축

소금, 우리는 부둥켜안고 서로의
몸속에서 바다를 채집하려 했다

오늘은 일어나자마자 염전이 문을 열었다
나는 아침부터 바다의 건축이 올라오는 소리 듣는다

나는 몸속에 입었다
소금 원피스 한 벌

我身體裏的鹽裙

如果忍受悲傷，身體裏會冒出鹽
你的表情鹹得令人不寒而慄
那是野獸的目光
猶如生生世世遭受大海打擊的孤島

短睫毛的籬笆之間
有時浪高，潮水洶湧
鹽的建築卻沒有倒塌
鹽花在指尖綻放，像熾熱的嗚咽

鹽。研磨我的倒影，撒在路燈之下
鹽。在我的身體裏遊轉的海的建築

鹽。我們緊緊擁抱，試圖
從對方的身體裏採集大海

今天剛起床，鹽店開門了
我從早晨就聽見大海建築上升的聲音

我在身體裏穿上
一套鹽裙

（薛舟　譯）

The Salt Dress Inside Me

When sorrow is endured, salt gets excreted from your body
Your salty-salty expression
Your animal gaze
like a lonely island hammered by the sea

Some days when there is a high-sea warning
seawater gushes in over the short eyelash fences
but the salt's architecture doesn't crumble
salt-flowers bloom from my fingertips like stinging sobs

Salt, turns my fallen shadow into powder and scatters it under the
streetlamps
Salt, persists in me like the sea's architecture

Salt, we embrace tightly and try
to capture the sea in each other

The salt pond is at work as soon as I'm awake
I listen to the rising sea architecture

I am wearing the salt dress
inside me

(Translated by Don Mee Choi)

인플루엔자

새라고 발음하면
내 몸에서 바람만 남고
물도 불도 흙도 다 사라지는 듯
그 이름 새는 새라는 이름의 질병인가
새는 종유석 같던 내 뼈에서 바람 소리가 나게 한다

날지 못하는 새들은 다 죽이라는 명령이 떨어졌다
죽일 새도 없으니 산 채로 자루에 넣어
구덩이에 파묻으라는 명령이 떨어졌다

나 시집와서 며칠 후 도마 위에 병아리를 올리고
그 털 벗은 것에 칼을 들어 내리치려할 때
갓 낳은 아기의 다리를 잡고 있던 기분
그 소름 돋은 것이 바들바들 떠는 것 같아
강보에 싸서 안아주고 싶었다

제 가슴을 베개 삼아 머릴 드리우고 잠들던 그것

정말 우리는 끝에 다 온 걸까?
악몽의 막이 찢기자 그 속에서 죽음이 탄생하고 있다

내 심장이 한 마리 바람처럼 박자 맞춰 떤다

우리 마을엔 이제 날개 달린 것이 없다
다 땅 속에 넣고 소독약을 뿌렸다

큰엄마는 기르던 거위를 포대기에 싸서
들춰 업으려다 방독면에 들켰다

내가 지금 새의 시를 쓰는 것은
새를 앓는다는 것
쇄골 위에 새 한 마리 올려놓고
부리로 쪼이고 있다는 것
사람이 죽으면 바람에 드는 것이라는데
나는 시방 새의 바람 속으로 든다

우리나라 하늘 연(鳶) 실이 다 엉켜
하늘 높이 쌓인 듯
흰 깃털 산이 바람에 힐끗거리고
그 속에 3 개월짜리 6 개월짜리 조그만 눈알들이
첩첩이 쌓여 있다
구덩이에 쏟아져 들어가기 몇 시간 전
눈 뜨고 떨고 있다

流感

當我說出「鳥」
身體裏彷彿只剩下風
水、火、土都消失了
莫非鳥是一種名字叫鳥的疾病？
鳥讓我鐘乳石般的骨頭發出風聲

我們受命殺死所有不會飛翔的鳥
因為來不及，命令又說裝進麻袋
活埋在土坑

出嫁幾天後，我把小雞放在菜板上
舉刀砍向被拔光毛的小東西
彷彿我抓著新生兒的腿
長滿雞皮疙瘩的牠在顫抖
我想把牠包進襁褓，抱在懷裏

那小東西枕著自己的胸膛打瞌睡

難道我們真的走到了絕境？
惡夢的膜被撕裂，死亡誕生

我的心臟像一縷風，跟著節拍顫抖

現在我們村裏沒有長翅膀的東西
牠們都被塞進泥土，灑上消毒液

伯母用襁褓包起家養的鵝
背在身上，卻被防毒面具揭穿

現在我正寫一首鳥的詩
這意味著鳥讓我疼痛
意味著一隻鳥棲息在我的鎖骨
啄我
他們說人死了會隨風而逝
可是我剛剛走進鳥的風

彷彿國家的風箏線相互糾纏
高高地堆滿天空
白色的羽毛山在風中窺視
那裏層層疊疊
堆積著三個月、六個月的眼珠
落坑前的幾個小時
牠們還睜著眼睛輕輕顫抖

（薛舟　譯）

Influenza

When I pronounce "bird"
only the wind remains in me
as if water, fire, earth all vanish
Maybe the name "bird" is the illness of the name "bird"
The bird makes the sound of blowing wind from my dripstone-like bones

We received an order to kill all the birds that couldn't fly
Since there was no time to kill, we received an order to put them in a sack
and bury them alive in a pit

A few days after I got married I placed a chick on a cutting board
and was about to strike the plucked bird with a knife
It felt as if I were holding the legs of a just-born infant
the chick covered in goose bumps was trembling
I wanted to wrap the bird in a baby's quilt and hold it in my arms

That thing that snoozes with its head pillowed on its chest

Have we really reached the end?
The nightmare's curtain rips and Death is born inside

Like a wall of wind my heart trembles to the rhythm

In my village now there are no such things with wings on them
They have all been put in the ground, powdered with disinfectant

My aunt was caught by Mr. Gas Mask
when she tried to wrap her goose in a baby blanket onto her back

The fact that I'm writing a bird poem means
that I'm ill with the bird
A bird perched on my collarbone
pecks me
They say when you die you go with the wind
but now I go with the wind of the bird

As if all the kite strings of my country have tangled and piled up high
in the sky
the white-feathered mountain flutters in the wind
and inside it 3-month old, 6-month old tiny eyes
heaped in layers
a few hours before they are shoved into the pit
they tremble with their eyes opened

(Translated by Don Mee Choi)

생일

아침에 눈 뜨면
침대에 가시가 가득해요
음악을 들을 땐
스피커에서 가시가 쏟아져요
나 걸어가면
발밑에 쌓이던 가시들
아무래도 내가 시계가 되었나봐요
내 몸에서 뾰족한 초침들이
솟아나나 봐요
그 초침들이
안타깝다
안타깝다
나를 찌르나 봐요
밤이 오면 자욱하게 비 내리는 초침 속을 헤치고
백 살 이백 살 걸어가 보기도 해요

저 먼 곳에
너무 멀어 환한 그 곳에
당신과 내가 살고 있다고
아주 행복하다고
당신 생일 날
그 초침들로 만든 케이크와 촛불로
안부 전해요

生日

早晨睜開眼睛
床上長滿了刺
聽音樂的時候
喇叭裏冒出刺
當我走路
腳下堆滿了刺
也許是我變成了鐘錶
我的身體裏冒出
鋒利的秒針
那些秒針
刺向我
你好可憐
你好可憐
夜晚我穿過細雨濛濛的秒針
走上一百年，二百年

遙遠的地方
遙遠到燦爛的地方
住著你和我
據說很幸福
你生日那天
我用秒針做成的蛋糕和蠟燭
為你祝福

（薛舟　譯）

Birthday

When I open my eyes in the morning
my bed is full of thorns
When I listen to music
thorns spill out from the speakers
When I walk
thorns pile up beneath my feet
I must have become a watch
Pointed second hands
protrude from my body
They needle me, saying
You poor thing
You poor thing
I walk through the second hands raining down at night
till I'm one hundred, two hundred years old

Over there faraway
so remote that the place shines out
that you and I live there
that we are very happy
I send you my regards
on your birthday
with cake and candles
made from those second hands

(Translated by Don Mee Choi)

토성의 수면

나 눈 감으면 내 그림자들 다녀오는 곳
그곳에서 나는 연기로 만든 허리띠를 두르네
내 영혼이 저녁 모기떼처럼 앵앵거리면
그림자들 초원의 사자떼처럼 우글거리고
오늘 나를 태우고 남은 재가 일어나 춤추는 곳

토성의 달은 60 개
그리하여 내 그림자는 60 개
물론 눈동자는 120 개
해가 뜨는지 마는지
눈을 다 떠보지도 못하네

그리하여 내 몸이 몇 개인지
몇 개가 더 죽을 수 있는지
땅은 물렁물렁하고 발걸음은 건들건들하고
공기는 끈적끈적하고 가슴은 우글우글하고
당신의 유령이 거미줄처럼 내 영혼을 채가는 곳

내가 나에게 명복을 빕니다
나는 죽은 몸들을 타고 앉아
남은 몸 몇 개를 재워보네
그리움도 자고 의심도 자고
아직 열지 못한 목구멍도 자고 다 잠들라

너는 죽어서 무엇이 되고 싶니?
나는 죽어서 테두리 없는 것이 될 거야!

계속해서 계속해서 달이 떠오르는 곳
두꺼운 이불로 내리눌러도
이빨이 삐죽삐죽 새어나오는 곳
가느다란 지평선에 거무튀튀한 사자들 걸터앉아
삐져나오는 야광 눈빛 자꾸만 자꾸만 감기는 곳
그곳의 그림자들과 다 이별하면 이곳의 내 몸무게와도 다 이별하
겠네

土星的安眠藥

閉上眼，那是影子們去過的地方
我在那兒繫著煙霧織成的腰帶
如果我的靈魂嗡嗡像傍晚的蚊群
影子們開始蠕動，像草原的獅群
今天，我燃燒過的灰燼翩翩起舞

土星有60顆月亮
所以我有60個影子
當然就有120隻瞳孔
無論太陽是否升起
我都不能完全睜開眼睛

所以我有幾個身體
幾個身體可以死
大地綿綿軟軟，腳步搖搖晃晃
空氣黏黏糊糊，心臟咕嘟咕嘟
你的幽靈像蛛網抓走我的靈魂

我為自己祈禱冥福
我坐在死去的身體上
哄睡剩下的幾個身體
思念睡了，懷疑睡了
從未敞開的喉嚨也睡了，都睡吧

你死以後想要變成甚麼？
我死以後渴望變得無邊無際！

月亮不停地不停地升起的地方
蒙著厚厚的被子
牙齒還在尖銳冒出的地方
黑黢黢的獅子們蹲坐在修長的地平線
總是不停地不停地關閉夜光閃爍的眼睛
如果告別那個地方的影子
還要告別我在這個地方的體重

（薛舟　譯）

Saturn's Sleeping Pill

A place where my shadows visit when I close my eyes
There, I put on a belt made of smoke
When my soul buzzes like the mosquitoes at night
my shadows swarm like a pride of lions on the plains
A place where my ashes get up and dance after I've been burnt today

Saturn has 60 moons
therefore, I have 60 shadows
I have 120 eyes, of course
I don't get to open all of my eyes
whether the sun rises or not

Therefore, how many bodies do I have?
How many more bodies can die?
The ground is soft-soft and my footsteps are limp-limp
The air is sticky-sticky and my heart heaves-heaves
A place where your ghost snatches my soul away like a spider web

I pray for my own soul
I sit on my dead bodies
and put to sleep a few remaining live bodies
Longings are asleep doubts are asleep
even the throats that have not yet opened are asleep all asleep

What do you want to be when you die?
I'm going to be something that has no borders
A place where the moons rise continuously continuously
A place where teeth poke-poke out
even if you press them down with a thick blanket
A place where the dark sooty lions perch on the faint horizon
their eyelids keep keep falling on the glowing rays from their eyes
When you part with the shadows there
you also part with the weight of my body here

(Translated by Don Mee Choi)

科科瑟，生於1972年，當代緬甸詩人。他現居維也納，用緬甸文和英文兩種語言寫作。他的第一本英文詩集《生為緬甸人》（2015）收錄從1996年被禁止發表的小詩集到2014年在比利時魯汶大學的近作。此外，他編輯和翻譯的《白骨呻吟：當代緬甸詩人十五家》（2013）由北伊利諾伊大學出版。

ko ko thett was born in 1972, and is a poet by choice and a Burman by chance. He currently lives in Vienna and writes in both Burmese and English. The poems in his first English-language collection, *The Burden of Being Burmese* (2015), range from "faddish sugar crystals," written in Burmese for his illegal campus chapbook at the Yangon Institute of Technology in 1996, to his most recent work "anxiety attack," constructed at the University of Leuven in 2014. Apart from his own work as a writer and translator, he is co-editor of the seminal volume *Bones Will Crow: 15 Contemporary Burmese Poets* (Northern Illinois University Press, 2013).

科科瑟

KO KO THETT

the burden of being *bama*

it's living on
sawdust and shrimp paste
to save for diamonds

it's being a lustrous luna
in a bamboo tube
thinking "how dainty i am!"

it's being a haystack fire
flaring suddenly
fading out swiftly

it's aching for the aunt
from the embrace of the mother

what's your key
majority in minor-c or minority in major-d
ceasefire in flat-b or cease-identity in sharp-g
give me a falsetto
let's improvise
no need for harmony

what would you choose
want, rage or ignorance
defeatism or maldevelopment
an increase in viral load or a decrease in internet speed
sexual preoccupation or self-denial
power cuts or power crazes
a bag of rice or an ounce of democracy
myopic blitheness, escapist wizardry and alchemy
syncretization of incompatibilities
internalization of irreconcilabilities
the four noble truths
the four oaths.........
....
....
the menu is endless
the die's been cast

your karma is you
life short
suffering tall
plenty of water
no fish, no fish at all

做緬族人的壓力

以鋸木屑和蝦醬
為生計
為了存錢買鑽石

作為一個竹筒內
光明的月神
想著「我是多麼精巧呢！」

作為乾草堆中的火
突然燃燒
迅速熄滅

在母親的懷抱中
為阿姨而感到疼痛

你是甚麼調？
主要是C 小調或少量D 大調
停火於B♭或終止身份於G♯
給我假音
不如即興
不需要和諧

你會選擇甚麼
渴望、憤怒或無知
失敗主義或發育不良
增加病毒上載量或減慢上網速度

入迷性愛或自我否定
權力約束或權力瘋狂
一袋大米或一盎司民主
短視樂天，逃避主義者的神乎其技與煉金術
不相容的相容
不能和解的內化
四聖諦
四弘誓願……
……………………………………………
………………………

無盡的選項單
死亡已經選上

你的業就是你
人生短暫
痛苦太大
許多水
沒有魚，簡直沒有魚

(鄭政恆　譯)

the rain maker

switch off the lights, turn the projector on
sit back and relax, let's enjoy the mirages
on *kayan* rice wine and cheese crackers

a few simple rules here
you may bite the hand that feeds you,
just don't feast on it
don't multitask if you don't know
how to run north for a southbound hare
don't kill two robins with one word
if you don't know how to lie to one of them
don't chew the shoes and the drapery
don't be a member of any poetic community

don't be a rose fancier
you don't want to be another down comforter
fine feathers are unfit for us humans
they make you too hot within
too cold without

look how the dormant underdog,
taken for granted rotten-dead,
has sprung back to life on *dukkha* media!

sickened with divided attention disorder
it jumps over the crown, chokes and
strangles the aristocratic order

the kingdom now needs a flea leap forward
the newly elected leader may be comely
just don't expect her to change the clime

isn't it fascinating?
how each and every cowry trapped in a hollowed-out bamboo
houses an entire symphony orchestra

造雨者

關燈，打開投影機
坐好放鬆，享受
長頸族米酒和芝士餅乾的幻覺

這裏有少許簡單的規則
你可以恩將仇報，
只是不可盡情享受
不要處理多項事務，如果你不知道
如何為向南行的野兔而向北行
不要用一個字，殺死兩隻知更鳥
如果你不知道如何向其中一隻説謊
不要咀嚼鞋子和布料
不要成為任何詩歌團體的一員

不要成為玫瑰愛好者
你不想成為另一個傷心的慰問者
精緻的羽絨不適合我們人類
它們讓你穿著太熱
沒有了就太冷

看看睡著的弱者，
想當然會爛死，
已經通過苦道反彈回人生！

患了注意力分散失調
它跳過冠冕，掐住和
勒死貴族的秩序

現在王國需要一隻跳蚤的躍進
新當選的領導人可能秀麗
只是不用希望她改變風土

是不是吸引呢？
每一個貝殼如何陷入容納了一整隊交響樂團的
挖空的竹子裏面

（鄭政恆　譯）

the boomtown

a bottle spins
a rat for protein
a snake rattles
pots and pans for a pawnshop
lunar face for the thoroughfare
rickshaw for the landing vehicle

a tadpole morphs into a mermaid
isn't she just another census entry
you don't want to be weighed down
by the food chain, lectures the dean,
hanging loose between two branches

no soup in a salt crystal
no lamp oil in a sand grain
no sum makes her night
no catch cools her day
no rain fills her ocean stomach
no holds barred for her banquet
no one knows what side they're on
in her flesh and faith and toes
no exasperation unbearable
no exile banishment

a nip at the wrong ear, game over
a turn into the wrong lane, you're dead

mahogany doesn't live in a tundra
ghost orchids don't grow in a desert
between winter and summer
spring is the suspender belt

neon trenches for canonical gospels, trains
loaded with final holdouts leave every second
transmigration passes available for non-nationals
how would you like to be wrapped

vicuña wool for your majesty
foliage for the naked

新興都市

瓶子旋轉
老鼠給予蛋白質
蛇響尾
鍋碗瓢盆給予典當鋪
月球面孔給予大街道
人力車給予陸上車輛

蝌蚪變種成為美人魚
她是不是只不過另一個人口普查登錄
你不想被食物鏈
壓倒，教訓學監，
兩條樹枝之間鬆動的懸掛

水晶鹽中沒有湯
沙粒中沒有燈油
沒有錢讓她入夜
沒有掠奪讓她白日降溫
沒有雨水填滿她如海洋的肚
沒有限制在她的宴會之中
沒有人知道他們是那一邊
在她的肉體、信念和腳趾之中
沒有忍受不了的激憤
沒有流亡驅逐

在錯誤的耳朵一夾，遊戲結束
轉進錯誤的車道，你就死定了

紅木並不生長在凍土
幽靈蘭並不生長在沙漠
冬天和夏天之間
春天是吊襪帶

霓虹燈的溝渠代替按照教規的福音，火車
裝滿了最後的堅持在任何一秒鐘駛去
輪迴轉世給非本國人民通行
你想如何被包裹著

小羊駝毛留給尊貴的您
葉子留給裸體的人

(鄭政恆　譯)

衣田・拉朗德，魁北克（加拿大）蒙特利爾詩人。1999 年以年僅廿歲之齡出版詩集《我是食人族》以及《仍是戰爭》，後者進入艾塔・特雷絲・聖一蘇比絲詩歌獎的決選名單，並在雅克琳・德利一莫崇詩歌獎評審中獲特別嘉許。2010 年出版的詩集《大自然的故事》獲得2011 年菲利斯一勒可樂詩歌獎。另著有詩集《漸老》(2011)、《暗巷》(2012)、《維維爾・克勞德》(2013) 等，後者獲得埃米爾・內里根詩歌獎以及蒙特利爾詩歌節獎。從2000 到2012 年，拉朗德一共獲得五次魁北克文藝協會獎金和一次加拿大藝術協會獎金。拉朗德曾任紐約的魁北克工作室駐留作家，亦參與過俄羅斯、印度及丹麥等地舉辦的國際詩歌節。

Étienne Lalonde, originally from Montreal, Quebec (Canada), released his first two poetry collections, *Je cannibale* and *C'est encore la guerre*, in 1999, at the age of twenty. *C'est encore la guerre* was a finalist for the Estuaire Terrasses Saint-Sulpice Prize for Poetry and also received a special mention for the Jacqueline Dery-Mochon Prize for Poetry. *Histoires naturelles*, published in 2010, was awarded the 2011 Felix-Leclerc Prize for Poetry. His critically acclaimed book *Devenir vieux* came out in 2011. In 2012, Lalonde published *Chemins mal éclairés* and, in 2013, *Vivier, Claude*, finalist for both the Émile-Nelligan and the Montreal Poetry Festival Prizes for Poetry. From 2000 to 2012, Lalonde received five grants from the Conseil des arts et des lettres du Quebec, as well as one from the Canada Council for the Arts. He was a writer-in-residence at the Quebec Studio in New York and has taken part in international poetry festivals in Russia, India and Denmark.

衣田・拉朗德

ÉTIENNE LALONDE

La douleur a ses secrets

En cela, même à genoux
Être beau comme un train

La douleur mange de tout
Elle a bien des secrets

Une odeur d'herbe coupée
Détruit tout ce matin

Les montagnes se désistent
Ou demeurent immobiles
Sur le point de tomber

Le silence doit alors
Émettre un signal
Entouré de chaleur

Écoute septembre dehors

Les arbres nus
Prennent des poses
Auxquelles le brouillard consent

憂傷也有秘密

在那裏面，甚至在膝蓋裏
英俊得如同一列火車

憂傷甚麼都吃
她也有不少秘密

剪草的氣味
今早殺死了一切

群山退後
或者變得靜止
即將跌倒

那麼寂靜必須
更改它的訊號
被熱力圍繞

在外傾聽九月

樹木赤裸著
擺出姿勢
為了霧的首肯

（黃峪　譯）

Grief has secrets

In that, even on bended knees
Being handsome like a train

Grief eats anything
It has many secrets

The scent of cut grass
Kills everything this morning

Mountains stand back
Or become motionless
About to tip over

Silence must then
Transmit its signal
Cushioned by heat

Listen to September outside

Trees naked
pose for
the consenting fog

(Translated by Hugh Hazelton and Antonio D'Alfonso)

Je pouvais aller vite

J'ai tremblé
Éclosion

J'ai éteint la lumière
Qui faisait non des yeux
Secouant chaque automne
Dans la chambre à démons

À heure fixe
J'ai attendu l'accident
Avec mon sommeil léger
Mon bruit pas tellement mieux
Plein de trous

Je pouvais aller vite
Lumière

Même quand je me réveillais
Sur les murs
Je me laissais couler
Avant de m'envelopper dans l'air

Dans la nuit
Du noir frais au rire fauve
Avec des éclairs

我本來可以走得更快

我顫抖
漸漸綻放

我熄了燈
它剛才正用眼睛說不
每個秋天都搖晃
在魔鬼的房間裏

正在這個時候
我聽到這場意外
而我正在淺睡
我的噪音也不見得更好
它佈滿穿孔

我本來可以走得更快
光亮

即使開始甦醒
在牆壁上
我也會讓自己滾滾
然後陷入空氣的懷抱

在夜裏
黑暗假笑得清涼
閃電劃過

（黃峪　譯）

I could have moved faster

I quivered
Blossoming

I shot the light off
Which was nodding no with its eyes
Shaking every autumn
In the devil room

At the right moment
I heard the accident
In my restless slumber
My noise no better
Riddled with holes

I could have moved faster
Flare

Even awakening
On walls
I would let myself roll down
And into an envelop of air

During the night
Darkness is cool with its musky smile
And lightning

(Translated by Hugh Hazelton and Antonio D'Alfonso)

Car le ciel était vrai

Puis, j'ai eu une étoile
Un nom, une collision

Car le ciel était vrai

Il n'était pas de moi

Échec, rideau, rappel

Les dimanches ont le dos large

Allez, imaginez
La nuit masquée maintenant

Une rue, un arbre, un trou

Noir cruel, étouffé

J'ai l'air fou, arraché

C'est peut-être pour mon bien

Un rire creux comme avant

因為天空曾經真實

那時我曾擁有一顆星星
一個名字，一次撞擊

因為天空曾經真實

它非我所有

失敗，窗簾，回憶

星期天慷慨大方

來吧，繼續想像
夜晚現在蒙上面具

一條路，一棵樹，一個洞

殘酷的黑，窒息了

我貌似瘋狂，被綁架

這可能對我更好

笑聲空洞一如過往

（黃峪　譯）

Because the sky was real

Then I was given a star
A name, a collision

For the sky was real

Did not belong to me

Failure, curtain, recall

Sundays are generous

Now, go on, imagine
The night with a mask

Street, tree, hole

Darkness cruel, smothered

I look mad, kidnapped

Maybe it's for my own good

Laughter as hollow as passing

(Translated by Hugh Hazelton and Antonio D'Alfonso)

Faire le ménage de ça

Les cris, l'après-midi
Faire le ménage de ça

L'air peut aller plus vite
Du revers de la main

Une plante en tant que voisin

L'heure a le droit de dire non

Au secours

Un cadre, un portrait

Qui peut hanter plus loin

Dérouter nos fantômes

打掃房間去吧

尖叫　下午
打掃房間去吧

空氣會流通得更快
把手翻轉之後

一棵植物當作鄰居

時間有權利說不

救救我

一副相框　一張肖像

能夠繼續縈繞

讓我們的鬼魂走上歧路

(黃峪　譯)

Need for house cleaning

The screaming, the afternoon
Need for house cleaning

Air moves faster
With back of hand

House plant as neighbor

The hour has the right to say no

Help me

A frame, a portrait

That could haunt the beyond

Leading our ghosts astray

(Translated by Hugh Hazelton and Antonio D'Alfonso)

飲江，原名劉以正，1949 年12 月生於香港，70 年代開始新詩創作，曾獲「香港青年文學獎」、「工人文學獎」、「職青文藝獎」及「香港中文文學獎」等詩歌創作獎項。1987 年與朋友創辦《九分壹》詩刊，並參與早期編輯工作。他歷任多屆「香港中文文學獎」詩歌獎評委，並多次參與「香港青年文學獎」、「工人文學獎」、「大學文學獎」、「秋螢詩獎」、「李聖華詩獎」等評審工作。其詩集《於是你沿街看節日的燈飾》於1997 年出版，並獲「香港中文文學雙年獎」。2010 年出版另一個較完整的詩集《於是搬石你沿街看節日的燈飾》，收錄有130 多首詩。

Lau Yee-ching, born in December 1949 in Hong Kong, started to write poetry in the 1970s. He has received the Hong Kong Youth Literature Award, Workers' Literature Award, and the Hong Kong Biennial Award for Chinese Literature. In 1987, he co-founded the poetry magazine *One-Ninth* with his friends, and was involved in editing the first few issues. Lau was appointed a referee for several poetry awards in Hong Kong including the Hong Kong Youth Literature Award, the Workers' Literature Award, and the Qiu Ying Poetry Award. His book of poems, *And So You Look at the Festive Lights along the Street* (1997), won the Hong Kong Biennial Award for Chinese Literature. In 2010, he published a more complete edition of this book, *And So, Roll the Stone, You Look at the Festive Lights along the Street*, which is a collection of more than 130 poems.

飲江

LAU YEE-CHING

創造者的眼睛

寫作的喜悅
保存的力量
人類之手的復仇
—— 辛波絲卡

這世界乃我所創造
但我未能目睹它的誕生
那重要時刻，你躡足
走來，伸手掩著我的眼睛

猜猜，我是誰

我猛然轉過身來
寧願讓我的受造物
各歸其位，或各自消遁
也要擁抱你，和被你擁抱

但，你是　誰呢
你那雙惡作劇的可愛的小手
此刻又掩著誰，那一位
創造者的眼睛

Creators' Eyes

The joy of writing
The power of preserving
Revenge of a mortal hand
—Szymborska

This world is my creation
yet I did not witness its birth
that crucial moment, you tiptoed
over, reached around and covered my eyes

Guess who

I whipped myself around
I would have my creations
each resume its place, or disparate
that I could hug you, and be hugged

But, who　are you
and who are your tricky, adorable little
hands blindering right now, that other
creator's eyes

(Translated by Canaan Morse)

行為藝術
——給媚

丹麥美人魚尋回失頭
又是我們郁手的時候

我們以生命
的虛無
成就她
永恆
的變奏

直至我們
也成為
銅像
或石頭
塗鴉者被塗鴉
在虛擬
的牆上
哭泣
的網上
像海妖
歌唱

像海妖
靜默時

那七種
歌唱

歌唱不被理解
的哀傷
和理解
尾隨

之遺忘

2000

Performance Art

—for Mei

Denmark's Little Mermaid found her head
it's time for us to act again

We accomplish her
eternal
syncopation
with the emptiness
of our existence

Until we also
turn into
bronze statues
or stone heads
vandals are vandalized
on a fictitious
wall
a weeping
web
like Sirens
singing

Like those seven
kinds of songs
when the Sirens
are silent

The sorrow of singing
without being understood
and the understanding
that's followed

by forgetting

2000

(Translated by Canaan Morse)

長者獨居

當那獨居的長者獨居
你還未出世
而今你是那獨居長者
獨自守著
那麼一個謎
彷彿是眷顧
更是懲罰
你不像別人的愛侶
捆縛炸藥離家遠去
也不像自己的戀人
和他從前的戀人
被驟來的炮呀火呀

或天上掉下來的 花樽　花瓣　花粉

摧毀

The Elder Lives Alone

When that lonely-living elder lived alone
you were not yet born
while today you are that elder
keeping solitary watch
over such a secret
it looks like affection
and more like punishment
You're not like other people's lovers
bundling gunpowder and leaving home
nor are you like your own lover
or his past lovers
obliterated
by sudden blasts or fire

or vases　petals　pollen falling

from heaven

(Translated by Canaan Morse)

陰謀不沾染的世界

作為陰謀家
活在沒有陰謀
這世界

其苦
可想
其樂
可想

作為陰謀家
陰謀不沾染世界
其樂可想
其苦
可想

親愛的
你就是
那個
可想

A World Uninfected by Conspiracy

As a conspirator
living in a world without
conspiracy

imagine
the frustration
imagine
the joy

as a conspirator
conspiracy doesn't infect the world
imagine the joy
imagine
the frustration

my dear
you are
that very
imagination

(Translated by Canaan Morse)

小花女

—— 給女兒丹丹

那交替著踮起腳尖的
小花女
把鮮花
撒在
自己的
婚禮上

這秘密
唱詩的
男孩知道
歌聲
格外
輕柔

Pretty Poppet

—for my daughter, Dandan

That pretty poppet
prancing on tiptoes
scatters flowers
over her
own wedding

This boy who
sings secret poems
knows
how exceedingly
gentle
the song

(Translated by Canaan Morse)

尼古拉・馬茲洛夫，詩人，散文家，譯者，1973年生於前南斯拉夫的馬其頓，出身於一個經歷過巴爾幹戰爭的難民家庭。他18歲時，南斯拉夫解體，文化身份發生了轉變。馬茲洛夫的詩歌被翻譯成四十種語言出版，其中《重置的石頭》（2007）曾贏得「Hubert Burda歐洲詩歌獎」，也曾在斯特魯加詩歌之夜獲得「米拉迪諾夫兄弟詩歌獎」，還獲得數個文學獎金，包括愛荷華大學「國際作家工作坊」、柏林「DAAD文學獎金」、法國「瑪格麗特・尤瑟娜文學獎金」等。馬茲洛夫也是*Lyrikline*詩歌網站的主持，常年四海為家。斯洛文尼亞詩人薩拉蒙曾對馬茲洛夫的詩作出如下評論：「馬茲洛夫創造高昂的沉默，把空間與和平重新灌注到力量之中。我們一直以來都追尋著這種純粹。」波蘭詩人扎加耶夫斯基亦有以下評論：「馬茲洛夫的詩就像表現主義的畫，有厚實而充滿活力的線條，似乎來自於想像，又立刻回到想像，就像夜晚被車燈照到的動物。」

Nikola Madzirov (poet, essayist, and translator) was born into a family of Balkan War refugees in Macedonia, ex-Yugoslavia, in 1973. When he was 18, the collapse of Yugoslavia prompted a shift in his sense of identity. There is a clear line connecting the generation of the East European poets like Czesław Miłosz, Zbigniew Herbert, Vasko Popa and Adam Zagajewski to Nikola Madzirov. However, Madzirov provides a new voice in 21st century European poetry and is one of the most outstanding poets of the post-Soviet generation. The German weekly magazine *Der Spiegel* has compared the quality of Madzirov's poetry to Tomas Tranströmer's. The Slovenian poet Tomaž Šalamun wrote: "Madzirov created loud silence. He brought back the space and peace to the power. There are times (now) when we long after exactly this kind of purity." The Polish poet Adam Zagajewski describes how "Madzirov's poems are like Expressionist paintings: filled with thick, energetic streaks they seem to emerge from the imagination and to return to it right away, like night animals caught in the headlights of a car." Madzirov's work has been translated into 40 languages. He is author of several books including *Relocated Stone* (2007), which received the Hubert Burda European Award. He won the Miladinov Brothers Award at the Struga Poetry Evenings and was granted the International Writing Program (IWP) fellowship at the University of Iowa, the DAAD fellowship in Berlin, and the Marguerite Yourcenar fellowship in France. Madzirov is one of the coordinators at the international poetry network *Lyrikline*. He spends his life in temporary homes.

尼古拉 · 馬茲洛夫

NIKOLA MADZIROV

СЕНКИТЕ НÈ ОДМИНУВААТ

Еден ден ќе се сретнеме,
како бротче од хартија и
лубеница што се лади во реката.
Немирот на светот ќе
биде со нас. Со дланките
ќе го помрачиме сонцето и со фенер
ќе се доближуваме.

Еден ден ветрот нема
да го промени правецот.
Брезата ќе испрати лисја
во нашите чевли пред прагот.
Волците ќе тргнат по
нашата невиност.
Пеперутките ќе го оставaт
својот прав врз нашите образи.

Една старица секое утро
ќе раскажува за нас во чекалната.
И ова што го кажувам е
веќе кажано: го чекаме ветрот
како две знамиња на граничен премин.

Еден ден сите сенки
ќе нè одминат.

陰影經過我們身邊

我們有天會再見面
就像一隻紙船和
一個在河水裏沁涼的西瓜。
這個世界的焦慮會
與我們同在。我們將
用手掌虧蝕太陽，
持著燈籠彼此靠近。

有一天，風不會
改變方向。
白樺樹將把葉子
送進門檻上我們的鞋子裏。
狼群將追捕
我們的純真。
蝴蝶將把牠們的粉塵
留在我們的臉頰上。

一個老婦人將述説故事
關於我們每個早晨在等候室裏
即使是我現在説的話
也已經被説過了：我們在等待風
就像邊境上的兩面旗幟。

有一天所有的陰影
　　　　都會從我們身邊經過。

（黃峪、Marija Todorova　譯）

Shadows Pass Us By

We'll meet one day,
like a paper boat and
a watermelon that's been cooling in the river.
The anxiety of the world will
be with us. Our palms
will eclipse the sun and we'll
approach each other holding lanterns.

One day, the wind won't
change direction.
The birch will send away leaves
into our shoes on the doorstep.
The wolves will come after
our innocence.
The butterflies will leave
their dust on our cheeks.

An old woman will tell stories
about us in the waiting room every morning.
Even what I'm saying has
been said already: we're waiting for the wind
like two flags on a border.

One day every shadow
　　　　will pass us by.

(Translated by Magdalena Horvat)

НЕ ЗНАМ

Далечни се сите куќи што ги сонувам,
далечни се гласовите на мајка ми што на
вечера ме повикува, а јас трчам кон полињата со жито.

Далечни сме ние како топка што го промашува голот
и оди кон небото, живи сме
како термометар кој е точен само тогаш кога
ќе погледнеме кон него.

Далечната стварност секој ден ме испрашува
како непознат патник што ме буди на половина пат
со прашање *„Тој ли е автобусот?"*,
а јас му велам *„Да"*, но мислам *„Не знам"*,
не знам каде се градовите на твоите дедовци
што сакаат да ги напуштат сите откриени болести
и лековите што содржат трпеливост.

Сонувам за куќа на ридот од нашите копнежи,
да гледам како брановите на морето го исцртуваат
кардиограмот на нашите падови и љубови,
како луѓето веруваат за да не потонат
и чекорат за да не бидат заборавени.

Далечни се сите колиби во кои се криевме од дождот
и од болката на срните што умираа пред очите на ловците
кои беа повеќе осамени, отколку гладни.

Далечниот миг секој ден ми поставува прашање
„Тој ли е прозорецот? Тој ли е животот?", а јас му велам
„Да", а всушност *„Не знам"*, не знам кога
птиците ќе прозборат, а да не кажат *„Небо"*.

我不知道

遙遠的是我夢想中的所有房子，
遙遠的是我母親的聲音
喚我吃晚飯，而我卻奔向那麥田。

我們遙遙相對就像一個錯過目標的球
飛向天際，我們活著
就像一個溫度計它僅僅在我們看著它的時候
讀數才準確。

這遙遠的現實每天都在和我對質
就像一個陌生的旅客在途中把我叫醒
説「請問是這部車麼？」
然後我回答「是的」，但其實我想説「我不知道」
我不知道你祖父母的城市
他們希望離開那裏發現的各種疾病
還有以耐心開展的治療方案。

我夢見在我們的慾望之山上有一所房子，
可以看見海浪怎樣描畫
一幅心電圖關於我們的失落和愛情，
看見人們如何相信以免於沉落
邁步以免於被忘卻。

遙遠的是保護我們免於風暴襲擊的那些小屋
在裏面我們免於體驗母鹿死亡的疼痛　牠們死在那些獵人的眼前
他們寂寞　但並不飢餓。

這遙遠的時刻每天都問我
「這是窗戶麼？」「這是生活麼？」我説
「是的」，但其實我想説「我不知道」，我不知道
鳥兒是否會開始説話，而不提到「天空」。

(黃峪、Marija Todorova　譯)

I Don’t Know

Distant are all the houses I am dreaming of,
distant is the voice of my mother
calling me for dinner, but I run toward the fields of wheat.

We are distant like a ball that misses the goal
and goes toward the sky, we are alive
like a thermometer that is precise only when
we look at it.

The distant reality every day questions me
like an unknown traveler who wakes me up in the middle of the journey
saying *Is this the right bus?,*
and I answer *Yes*, but I mean *I don't know,*
I don't know the cities of your grandparents
who want to leave behind all discovered diseases
and cures made of patience.

I dream of a house on the hill of our longings,
to watch how the waves of the sea draw
the cardiogram of our falls and loves,
how people believe so as not to sink
and step so as not to be forgotten.

Distant are all the huts where we hid from the storm
and from the pain of the does dying in front of the eyes of the hunters
who were more lonely than hungry.

The distant moment every day asks me
Is this the window? Is this the life? and I say
Yes, but I mean *I don’t know*, I don't know if
birds will begin to speak, without uttering *A sky*.

(Translated by Peggy and Graham W. Reid)

ИЗРЕЧЕНОТО НÈ ПРОГОНУВА

Им дадовме имиња
на дивите растенија
зад недовршените згради,
ги именувавме сите споменици
на нашите поробувачи.
Децата ги крстивме
со љубовните прекари
извлечени од писмата
еднаш прочитани.

Отпосле тајно ги толкувавме потписите
на дното од рецептите
за неизлечиви болести,
со двоглед ги зближувавме дланките
на простување потпрени
врз прозорците.

Зборовите ги остававме
под камењата со закопани сенки,
на ридот кој го чува ехото
на предците што не се впишани
во семејното стебло.

Она што го кажавме без сведоци
уште долго ќе нè прогонува.

Зимите се намножија во нас
без да бидат спомнати.

我們說過的話陰魂不散

我們給這些生長在
未完工樓房後面的
野生植物
起了名字，
給我們侵略者的所有紀念銅像
起了名字。
我們為自己的孩子們
起親暱的小名
選自僅讀過一次的
書信裏。

然後我們秘密地闡釋
處方頁尾的簽名
為了不治之症，
戴著望遠鏡我們拉近焦距
看那些在窗邊招展的手
說著告別。

我們把話語
留在石頭下面同被葬的影子一起
留在守護回聲的山上
留給我們的祖先而他們的名字
不在家族樹裏。

我們在沒有證人時說的話
總是陰魂不散。
在我們裏面堆疊著幾許冬季
根本沒人提及。

(黃峪、Marija Todorova　譯)

What We Have Said Haunts Us

We've given names
to the wild plants
behind unfinished buildings,
given names to all the monuments
of our invaders.
We've christened our children
with affectionate nicknames
taken from letters
read only once.

Afterwards in secret we've interpreted
signatures at the foot of prescriptions
for incurable diseases,
with binoculars we've zoomed in
on hands waving farewell
at windows.

We've left words
under stones with buried shadows,
on the hill that guards the echo
of the ancestors whose names are not
in the family tree.

What we have said without witnesses
will long haunt us.
The winters have piled up in us
without ever being mentioned.

(Translated by Peggy and Graham W. Reid)

ПРЕД ДА СЕ РОДИМЕ

Улиците беа асфалтирани
пред да се родиме и сите
соѕвездија веќе беа формирани.
Лисјата гниеја
до работ на тротоарот.
Среброто црнееше врз
кожата на работниците.
Нечии коски растеа низ
должината на сонот.

Европа се обединуваше
пред да се родиме и косата
на една девојка спокојно
се ширеше врз површината
на морето.

在我們出生之前

街道鋪上了瀝青
在我們出生之前，所有的
星群已經形成。
樹葉正在腐爛
在人行道的邊上
銀子變得黯然無光
在工人的皮膚上
某人的骨頭一路生長著穿過
睡夢的長度。

歐洲正在統一
在我們出生之前
一個少女的頭髮散開
冷冷然在海的
表面

（黃峪、Marija Todorova　譯）

Before We Were Born

The streets were asphalted
before we were born and all
the constellations were already formed.
The leaves were rotting
on the edge of the pavement,
the silver was tarnishing
on the workers' skin,
someone's bones were growing through
the length of the sleep.

Europe was uniting
before we were born and
a woman's hair was spreading
calmly over the surface
of the sea.

(Translated by Peggy and Graham W. Reid)

艾赫・米索，以色列著名詩人，創意寫作教師。1946年出生於外西凡尼亞，其父母是奧斯維辛集中營的生還者，1950年跟隨父母遷往以色列。米索出版了16本詩集，其中兩本是回顧集，分別出版於2003和2015年。她的詩曾被改編成音樂，並翻譯成多國語言出版，包括《Look There》（英文）、《Journal du verger》（法文）、《Ropa Tendida》（西班牙文）以及《Şheherezada》（羅馬尼亞文）等。米索曾獲得總理獎、阿米亥詩歌獎等多個獎項。2015年，她被提名為特拉維夫大學榮譽博士，獲取意大利「勒里奇皮亞詩歌獎」。米索居住在特拉維夫的一個農莊。她在耶路撒冷大學取得碩士學位，後於特拉維夫大學和耶路撒冷希伯來大學教創意寫作，目前擔任特拉維夫「赫利孔」詩歌學校校長。

Agi Mishol is an established Israeli poet and creative writing teacher. She was born in Transylvania in 1946 to Hungarian Holocaust survivors who came to Israel in 1950. She holds a master's degree from the Hebrew University of Jerusalem and has taught creative writing at Tel Aviv University and the Hebrew University. Mishol has published sixteen volumes of poetry, including two retrospective collections of her work published in 2003 and in 2015. Some of her poems have been set to music and others translated into many languages, including *Look There* (in English, by Graywolf Press), *Journal du verger* (in French, by Caratères), *Ropa Tendida* (in Spanish, by Poesía Mayor), and *Şheherezada* (in Romanian, by Institutul Cultural Român). Mishol has received the Prime Minister's Award, the Yehuda Amichai Prize and many other awards. This year, she was nominated by Tel Aviv University as Doctor Philosophiae Honoris Causa and received the Lerici-Pea prize in Italy. Mishol is currently the director of the "Helicon" school of poetry in Tel Aviv. She lives in an agricultural community.

艾棘 · 米索

AGI MISHOL

אז

כְּשֶׁאָהַבְנוּ לְלֹא שׁוּלַיִם וֶאֱלוֹהִים
בָּא לָקַחַת אֶת שֶׁלּוֹ
זָרַקְנוּ לוֹ חִיּוּךְ קָטָן כִּי לֹא חָשַׁבְנוּ
שֶׁמַּגִּיעַ לוֹ יוֹתֵר

בּוֹהִים לְמֶרְחַקִּים אֲרוּכִּים בָּטַחְנוּ אָז
בַּאֲשִׁישׁוֹת:
חֲבִיתִיּוֹת אַהֲבָה קְטַנּוֹת מְטֻגָּנוֹת
לְשֶׁבַע הַשָּׁנִים
הַטּוֹבוֹת

מַפְסִידִים כְּנָפַיִים הַצּוֹמְחוֹת
רַק לְמִי שֶׁקּוֹדֶם קוֹפֵץ
אֶל הַתְּהוֹם
בִּלְעָדֵיהֶן.

當時

當我們愛得無邊無際，上帝
來拿他應得的
我們扔給他一個輕輕的微笑因為我們覺得
他不值更多

凝視著遙遠的距離，當時我們相信
愛的蛋糕：
小塊油炸薄餅
渴望七載豐年

失去生長出的翅膀
只為那第一個跳入
深淵的人
沒有他們

（林婧　譯）

Back Then

When we loved without margins and God
came to take his due we threw him a faint smile
thinking he deserved
no more.

Long distance gazers, we put our trust in cakes of love:
little fried crepes
of lust
for the seven
good years

forfeiting wings that grow
only for those who first jump
into the abyss
without them.

(Translated by Lisa Katz)

בגידה

כָּל גִּבְעוֹלֵי הַחַמְצִיץ שֶׁמָּצַצְתִּי
לֹא גִּלּוּ דָּבָר.

מִלִּים נֶעֶרְמוּ מֵאֲחוֹרֵי גַּבִּי
לְגִבְעָה יְרֻקָּה,
שִׁיפוֹת זָרְמוּ בְּמַעֲלֵה הַגְּזָעִים
וְזַרְעֵי הַתּוּרְמוּס בְּחֶשְׁכַּת הָאֲדָמָה
זָמְמוּ אֶת הַכָּחֹל.

גַּם אִם אֵין צוּרַת יָחִיד לְדֶשֶׁא
וְרַק הָרַבִּים עוֹשֶׂה יָרֹק
לֹא יָכוֹלְתִּי לָדַעַת.

יַעַר בִּירְנֶם הֵחֵל לָזוּז,
אַחַר כָּךְ הַמַּחֲשָׁבוֹת הֶחֱשִׁיכוּ
עִם כֹּל מָה שֶׁמֵּאֲחוֹרֵי הָעֵצִים.

背叛

我吮吸過的所有酢漿草莖
一無所獲

我背後的詞語堆砌
成一座綠色小山
韌皮流入了樹幹
羽扇豆的種子在泥土的黑暗中
密謀靛藍

縱然青草並無唯一模樣
唯有繁複方能化身為綠
我無從知曉

貝爾訥姆的森林開始移動
在那之後思想
與一切隱於樹後之物
變得黯淡無光

（林婧　譯）

Betrayal

All the sorrel stalks I sucked on
revealed nothing.

Words piled up behind my back
until they turned into a green hill.
Phloem coursed through the trunks;
lupine seeds plotted blue in the dark soil.

Even if there is no singular form for grass
and only the plural makes it green,
I could not have known.

Birnam Wood began to move,
afterwards thought darkened
with all that lay behind the trees.

(Translated by Joanna Chen)

בֵּין הָעֵצִים וְהַלֹּא עֵצִים

לֹא נוֹסַעַת לְשׁוּם מָקוֹם.
אֲנִי רְעוּעָה מִכְּדֵי לַעֲקֹר
מֵהֶקְשֵׁרַי
וְהָעַצְלוּת שֶׁבִּי שׁוֹאֶפֶת לְהַתְמִיד
בְּמַצָּבָהּ,
לְהַמְשִׁיךְ וְלִשְׁכֹּן בְּמֶרְחָבָהּ הַמֻּכָּר
לִפְנוֹת עֶרֶב
עַל הַמַּדְרֵגָה
כְּשֶׁהַדִּמְיוֹן שָׂבֵעַ
וְעֵינֵי הַצַּיָּדוֹת נָחוֹת כְּבָר
בְּגֻמְחוֹת רֹאשִׁי.

מָה אָקוּם פִּתְאוֹם אֵלֵךְ
אָבוֹא אֶבְחַשׁ
בִּגְלַל פַּרְדֵּס בָּשׂוּם שֶׁאֶת נְשִׁימָתוֹ
אֲנִי נוֹשֶׁמֶת -

דֶּקֶל וְיָשֶׁר מוֹחֵק מִשְׁמֶשֶׁת הַשָּׁמַיִם
מִלִּים שֶׁנִּשְׁאֲרוּ אַחֲרֵי שֶׁהָאַהֲבָה הָלְכָה
וְגַם הָעוֹרְבִים אֶחָד אֶחָד נִרְגָּעִים
לְתוֹךְ הַבְּרוֹשׁ כְּמוֹ הַדָּם
לְתוֹךְ הַשֶּׁקֶט,

הַמַּחֲשָׁבָה אֵינָהּ חוֹמֶדֶת
אֶת תְּכָנֶיהָ
וַאֲנִי רַק הֹוָה פֹּה
בֵּין הָעֵצִים וְהַלֹּא עֵצִים

דַּלְתִּי פְּתוּחָה לִרְוָחָה
וְהַלַּיְלָה הָרַךְ מְזֻמָּן לְתוֹךְ הַבַּיִת -

在樹與非樹之間

我甚麼地方都不去
我搖搖晃晃
無法從語境中自拔
我的懶惰渴望著
一成不變，
繼續居住在它熟悉的曠野
轉向傍晚
樓梯之上
當想像力飽足
我捕獵的雙眼已在
頭腦的壁櫃中休憩

我為何突然醒來
來你這裏鼓動你
因為一個芬芳果園
我曾呼吸它的氣息

筆直的椰棗樹從天空玻璃抹去
愛情走後話兒仍舊留存
烏鴉也一隻一隻的安靜下來
在血一般的柏樹之間
在靜謐之間，
思想並不渴求
它的內容
而我只在這裏出現
在樹與非樹之間

我的大門向安逸打開
歡迎這個柔軟的夜晚進入家裏

（林婧　譯）

Between the Trees and the non-Trees

I'm not going anywhere.
I'm too dilapidated to be moved
out of context,
and my laziness tends to stay
where it is,
settling down in a familiar space
at evening,
on the steps,
imagination sated,
my hunting eyes resting
in the sockets of my head.

Why should I get up,
come and go,
stir things up
because of a perfumed orchard
whose breath
I inhale—

Palm fronds wipe away
from the sky's windshield
the words remaining when love has gone
and the ravens too relax one by one
inside the cypress
like blood inside silence.

Thought doesn't covet
its contents.
I just
am here
between the trees and the non-trees,

my door wide open,
the soft night beckoned into the house.

(Translated by Joanna Chen)

עצה

קְחִי נְשִׁימָה וְהַתְחִילִי לְהִתְרַחֵק:
הַיָּרֵחַ
הַמַּאֲדִים
צְבִיר כּוֹכָבִים
הִלָּתוֹ הַחֲלָבִית שֶׁל הָחוֹמֶר הָאָפֵל

מִשָּׁם עֲשִׂי אֶת דַּרְכֵּךְ לְאַט
חֲזָרָה:

הַקַּסְיוֹפֵּיאָה
זְנַב דֻּבָּה קְטַנָּה
אוֹקְיָנוֹסִים, יַבָּשׁוֹת

כַּדּוּר הָאָרֶץ
עִם מִמְרַח הָאֱנוֹשׁוּת הָעוֹטֵף אוֹתוֹ -
הַקְּרוּם הַחַשְׁמַלִּי הָרוֹחֵשׁ

וְעַכְשָׁיו, עַל כִּסֵּא הָעֵץ
בְּחַדְרֵךְ
אִמְרִי לְעַצְמֵךְ שׁוּב:
לֹא צִטְטוּ אוֹתִי נָכוֹן,
דְּבָרַי הוּצְאוּ מֵהֶקְשֵׁרָם.

建議

你吸一口氣，去遠方：
月球
火星
星團
暗物質形成的乳白光暈

從那裏，你慢慢往回走：
仙后座
小母熊的尾巴
海洋，陸地

地球
包裹著一層人類漿糊
電力表皮沙沙作響

那麼現在，坐在你房間裏的
木頭椅子上，
再對你自己説一遍：
他們曲解了我的意思，
我的話被斷章取義。

（林婧　譯）

Advice

Take a breath and pull away:
to the moon,
to Mars,
to the galaxies,
the milky halo of dark matter.

Once there, make your way back slowly:
Cassiopeia,
the tail of the Little Bear
oceans, continents,

the Earth,
spread with a layer of mankind,
buzzing with electricity.

Then, on a wooden chair
in your room,
repeat to yourself:
my words were taken out of context.
I was misquoted.

(Translated by Joanna Chen)

שפת אם

הַשְּׁכֵנָה שֶׁמָּשְׁכָה אוֹתִי הַחוּצָה
וְחָתְכָה אוֹתִי מִמֵּךְ
אָמְרָה וַדַּאי: זֹאת יַלְדָּה!

אָבִי לִוָּה אָז סֶרֶט אִלֵּם
בַּפְּסַנְתֵּר הַיָּשָׁן בְּבֵית הַקּוֹלְנוֹעַ
וַאֲנִי גָּמַעְתִּי אוֹתָךְ מִיָּד,
מְחַפֶּשֶׂת אוֹתִי עַל הַמָּסָךְ הַמְּשֻׁלָּג
שֶׁל עֵינַיִךְ.

שֶׁמֶשׁ סְתָוִית זָרְחָה אָז
בְּסִילַדְצֶ׳ה,
צוֹעֲנִיָּה גִּלְּתָה לָךְ תְּמוּרַת אַוָּז
שֶׁאֶרְאֶה לַמֶּרְחָק
אֲבָל אִישׁ לֹא הֵבִין מָה נִבְּאָה הָאָלֶף הַקְּמוּצָה
שֶׁצָּרַחְתִּי חָזָק לְתוֹךְ הַחֶדֶר.

אַחֲרֵי זֶה הִתְכַּוַּצְתְּ לַאֲגוּדָל
שֶׁבִּמְקוֹמוֹ מָצַצְתִּי מַחַק
שֶׁל עִפָּרוֹן
עַד שֶׁהֲפַכְתִּי אוֹתוֹ

וְהִתְחַלְתִּי לִכְתֹּב
שִׁירָה
שֶׁחָזְרָה לִהְיוֹת לִי
אֵם.

母語

那個鄰居把我拉
把我與你割斷
她肯定地說：是個女孩！

當時我的父親在給一部默片伴奏
用影院裏的那部老舊的鋼琴
而我立刻把你啜飲了下去
你的眼睛是一片白雪覆蓋的螢幕
在上面尋找我

當時秋日的太陽高照
在西拉查
一個吉普塞女人為你揭示了鵝的回報
好讓我遠遠地看著
可是沒人明白縮寫的字母A 預言了甚麼
我朝著房間用力大喊

在這之後，你縮小成了拇指
我吮吸鉛筆橡皮以替代它
直到我變成了它
並開始寫作
一首詩歌
詩裏説換我成了
母親。

(林婧　譯)

Mother Tongue

The neighbor who pulled me out,
who cut me away from you,
likely said: It's a girl!

I gulped you down
right away, searching
for myself
on the snowy screen
of your eyes. My father
meanwhile accompanied
a silent movie on an old piano
in a cinema.

An autumn sun was shining
in Szilagycseh.
In exchange for a goose,
a gypsy revealed I would see far
but no one understood
the prophetic ahh,
the lingering *aleph* I screamed into the room.

Later you shrivelled into a thumb
that became an eraser
atop a pencil
that I sucked on until I turned it
around and began to write

poetry
that returned to me
as mother.

(Translated by Joanna Chen)

水田宗子，著名詩人和女性學批評家。水田宗子在東京女子大學文理學部畢業後，赴耶魯大學留學並取得美國文學博士學位。先後在美國多所大學任教，1985 年為創建城西短期大學回國，1992 年創立城西國際大學。著有詩集《歸路》、《聖塔芭芭拉的暑假》、《綠藻之海》等。評論集有《從女主人公到英雄——女性的自我與表現》、《20 世紀的女性表現——朝向性差異的外部》、《語言紡織羽衣——女性的行旅物語》、《現代主義思潮與「戰後女性詩歌」的發展》、《大庭美奈子的記憶文學》以及英文專著《埃德加·愛倫·坡的世界——罪與夢》、《近代日本文學中的現實與虛構》等。水田宗子翻譯有多部童話集和女性批評專著。她曾獲得瑞典駐東京大使館主辦的馬丁松國際詩歌獎，也被匈牙利政府授予共和國文化勳章，並獲世界數十所大學頒授名譽博士和名譽教授，現為日本城西大學理事長。

Noriko Mizuta's free-verse poetry has blended transnational feminist perspectives with meditations on the meaning of family and home through five decades. Mizuta joined the Boomerang Society poetry circle when she was an undergraduate in Japan. She then continued writing in the U.S., publishing *End of Spring* (1976) and *Interlude* (1980), and co-authored *Amber in Flames* (1996) with Ohba Minako, while living in Riverside, California. Mizuta returned to Japan in 1985, and published her major critical works of modern Japanese women writers. She has established together with Chinese poets the Japan-China Association for Short Poetry. Mizuta has also translated works by Sylvia Plath, Anne Sexton, and E. Ann Kaplan into Japanese. In 2009, she founded the poetry journal *Carillon Street*. Recent collections have included *The Road Home* (2008); the three-part *Summer Holidays in Santa Barbara* (2010), *A Wedding in Amsterdam* (2013), *Sabbath in Tokyo* (2015), and *Sea of Blue Algae* (2013), which explores themes of the life-cycle, humans' origins and destinations, and the acceptance of mourning. In 2013, Mizuta received the Cikada Prize, founded to commemorate Swedish poet and Nobel laureate, Harry Martinson.

水田宗子

NORIKO MIZUTA

深い眠りがあったら

深い眠りがあったら
目覚めてくるものがあろうに
季節が移れば
野の草も蕾を付けてくるように

列車に乗っているならば
後ろにおいていくものものに
別れの一瞥をなげかければいい
河の土手に立ちすくんでいた男
踏切で手をつないでいた幼い兄弟

すべては一瞬の決別
後ろに過ぎ去って行くスピードは
わたしの脚では
取り戻しに走れない

微睡んでいるのは
深い円筒の中
まわりながら
滑りながら
どこまで行っても不十分な
落下
底なしの誘惑
奈落まで落ちる覚悟でも
辿り着けない
傷口へ

目覚めが頼りの
願望
微睡んでいるのは谺の中
無すら反復する深い幻の谷間
霧の中から
還り続ける
音無しの音
過ぎ去らぬ時のエコー

如若沉睡

如若沉睡
總有甚麼會來喚醒
正如時光荏苒
野草也會長出花蕾

如若搭乘列車
向車尾消逝的一切
投上離別的一瞥便已足夠
河堤上呆立不動的男子
道口上牽著手年幼的兄弟

一切都是一瞬間的訣別
向後退去的速度
我的雙腳
無法追回

假寐
是在深深的圓筒中
繞啊繞
滑啊滑
到哪裏都不滿意
墜落
無底的誘惑
連一落到底的覺悟都
無法到達
向傷口
許下清醒藉以仰仗的
願望
假寐是在回聲中
連「無」都會反復的幻覺之深谷
從霧裏
不斷回歸的
無聲之聲
——無法成為過去的時間回聲

(田原、毛乙馨　譯)

If You Happen into a Deep Sleep

If you happen into a deep sleep,
An awakening will certainly follow,
Just as when the seasons change
And the field grasses put forth new buds

If you're riding on a train,
It's fine to send parting glances back
Toward all the things you leave behind
A man standing transfixed on a river embankment
Young siblings holding hands at a railway crossing

Everything is a momentary farewell
The speed of things disappearing behind,
I cannot reverse
Cannot run back to regain

Drifting off to sleep,
In a deep cylinder
Spinning away
Slipping away
Not enough, no matter how far it goes
Dropping
Bottomless temptation
Resolved to fall even to the underworld,
Never arriving
At the wound

Awakening's reliable
Aspiration
What is drifting to sleep amidst echoes
Reverberating nothing through the deep phantom valley
Out of the mist
Making its way home
Soundless sound
Never departing, echo of time

(Translated by Jordan A. Yamaji Smith)

青の詩

記憶が薄れていく先は
青い空
野原に寝転んで行く先を追う
青が終わるところに昔があるのか
青が虚ろになるところは
白いナッシング
闇でないのがいい
空はすっぽりとあたりを包み
草原いっぱいの忘却
どこにも手がかりはない

わたしは
薄れた記憶を吸い込む
味のない
青

藍之詩

記憶褪色的前方
是藍天
橫躺在草原去追趕那前方
藍的盡頭難道還有往昔？
在藍成為空洞之際
只有白色的虛無
不是黑暗就已足夠
天空覆蓋周圍
草原充滿忘卻
不論哪裏都茫無頭緒

我
吸入褪色的記憶
和無味的
藍

（田原、毛乙馨　譯）

Poem in Blue

Where memory goes fading on
Blue sky
Tumbling to the field, I follow
Where the blue ends, could long-ago be there?
Where blue goes blank
A white nothing
Better yet, a not-darkness
Sky envelops everything around
A meadow's worth of oblivion
Nowhere so much as a trace

I
Inhale that faded memory
Flavorless
Blue

(Translated by Jordan A. Yamaji Smith)

紫陽花—庭6

梅雨前線に異常があって
紫陽花は青空の下で咲いている
照りつける日差しの中で
色を変える暇もなく
変身し遂げる余裕もなく
祭りをもりたてもしないで
一直線に満開

急がないで
急がないで
それでもあじさいは花
急いでも急がなくても
今年は終わり

紫陽花—庭院 6

梅雨前線發生了異常
紫陽花在晴空下綻放
毒曬的日光裏
既無暇變色
也無力變身
更不為節日添色
一直盛開

不用急
不用急
即使如此，紫陽花依然是花
無論急還是不急
今年到此為止

（田原、毛乙馨　譯）

Hydrangeas—*Garden* 6

Rather odd for the season of early summer rains
Hydrangeas, blooming under blue sky
Under the all-illuminating sunshine
No time for their color to deepen,
Too rushed for a full transformation
Without quite livening up the festival,
They burst into full blossom

Don't hurry
Don't hurry
But hydrangeas are after all a flower
Whether they hurry or not
This year will end

(Translated by Jordan A. Yamaji Smith)

萊斯・馬雷，著名澳洲詩人，生於1938年10月，1965年開始發表詩歌，至今出版超過16本詩集。他居住在新南威爾士州本雅鄉的農場，即是他出生的地方。馬雷的詩曾被翻譯成德文、荷蘭文、丹麥文、挪威文、瑞典文、法文、意大利文、斯洛文尼亞文、馬其頓文和西班牙文等，在世界各地出版，並贏得許多國際詩歌獎，包括「格蕾絲利文詩歌獎」、「皮特拉克詩歌獎」、「英國皇后詩歌金章」、「T. S. 艾略特詩歌獎」、「意大利蒙德約國際詩歌獎」等。在馬雷的作品中，衝突的主題多出現於早年他在城市時寫的詩，回歸鄉野後，他嘗試抵抗都市題材的誘惑。

Les Murray, born October 1938, is a prominent Australian poet who has published 16 poetry collections since 1965. He lives on a small former farm at Bunyah, the rural district in which he grew up. Some of his collections have been published in translation, notably in German, Dutch, Danish, Norwegian, Swedish, French, Italian, Slovenian, Macedonian and Spanish, and he has won notable prizes in several of the listed languages. Prominent prizes in English that have come his way home have included the Petrarch Prize, the T. S. Eliot Prize, Queen's Gold Medal for Poetry and the Mondello Prize in Italy. Conflict is a diminishing theme in his writing, and plays a lesser role now than in earlier years, being set aside very largely by subjects of rural life and the Lord. He has tended to resist urgings to concentrate on urban subjects.

萊斯·馬雷

LES MURRAY

The Gum Forest

After the last gapped wire on a post,
homecoming for me, to enter the gum forest.

This old slow battlefield: parings of armour,
cracked collars, elbows, scattered on the ground.

New trees step out of old: lemon and ochre
splitting out of grey everywhere, in the gum forest.

In there for miles, shade track and ironbark slope,
depth casually beginning all around, at a little distance.

Sky sifting, and always a hint of smoke in the light;
you can never reach the heart of the gum forest.

In here is like a great yacht harbour, charmed to leaves,
innumerable tackle, poles wrapped in spattered sail,
or an unknown army in reserve for centuries.

Flooded-gums on creek ground, each tall because of each.
Now a blackbutt in bloom is showering with bees
but warm blood sleeps in the middle of the day.

The witching hour is noon in the gum forest.
Foliage builds like a layering splash: ground water
drily upheld in edge-on, wax-rolled, gall-puckered
leaves upon leaves. The shoal life of parrots up there.

Stone footings, trunk-shattered. Non-human lights.
Enormous abandoned machines. The mysteries of the gum forest.

Delight to me, though, at the water-smuggling creeks,
health to me, too, under banksia candles and combs.

A wind is up, rubbing limbs above the bullock roads;
mountains are waves in the ocean of the gum forest.

I go my way, looking back sometimes, looking round me;
singed oils clear my mind, and the pouring sound high up.

Why have I denied the passions of my time? To see
lightning strike upward out of the gum forest.

桉樹林

走過通電鐵線欄的最後一根木柱，
回家，對我而言，就是走入那片桉樹林。

這片古老而緩慢的戰場：裝甲刨花，
護領護肘均破裂，散落在四周。

新樹踏著老樹簇湧而出：在這片桉樹林
灰色無處不在，分裂出檸檬色和赭紅色。

樹蔭小徑和鐵皮樹山坡綿延數英哩，
景深處處，始於距離稍遠的地方。

天空在篩濾，日光中總有煙靄隱約；
永遠無法達到桉樹林的心臟地帶。

於此彷彿置身於遊艇港灣，著迷於葉帆、
數不盡的索具，濺污的帆布裹著桅桿，
就像一支被養了幾個世紀的無名軍隊。

溪地上被浸淹的桉樹，競相拔高。
一棵茂盛的黑基木樹撒下一襲蜜蜂
但是正午時，溫暖的血液正在沉睡。

桉樹林裏，正午是魅惑的時刻。
葉叢疊疊，猶如層層濺灑：地面的水潭
在乾燥中苦撐，葉子輕壓葉子，
微醉，被蠟卷過，被蟲瘻蛀過。樹上鸚鵡群立而生。

樹腳鋪滿石頭，樹幹已破碎。不是人造的光。
巨大的機器被廢置於此。桉樹林的玄奧。

溪流偷運水源，但是於我是愉悦，
站在猶如蠟燭和髮梳的班克西花下，於我是健爽。

一陣風起於闇牛道上，揉擦牠們的四肢；
在桉樹林之海，山巒即是海浪。

我走著自己的路，時不時回頭，環顧四周；
油輕微燎焦，讓我頭腦清淨，頭頂上還有傾瀉的聲音。

為何我拒絕生活的歡情？要看看
閃電如何從這片桉樹林煉擊天空。

(宋子江　譯)

Dead Trees in the Dam

Castle scaffolding tall in moat,
the dead trees in the dam
flower each morning with birds.

It can be just the three resident
cormorants with musket-hammer necks, plus
the clinician spoonbill, its long pout;

twilight's herons who were almost too lightfoot
to land; pearl galahs in pink-fronted
confederacy, each starring in its frame,

or it may be a misty candelabrum
of egrets lambent before saint Sleep—
who gutter awake and balance stiffly off.

Odd mornings, it's been all bloodflag
and rifle green: a stopped-motion shrapnel
of kingparrots. Smithereens when they freaked.

Rarely, it's wed ducks, whose children
will float among the pillars. In daytime
magpies sidestep up wood to jag pinnacles

and the big blow-in cuckoo crying
Alarm, Alarm on the wing is not let light.

This hours after dynastic charts of high

profile ibis have rowed away to beat
the paddocks. Which, however green, are
always watercolour, and on brown paper.

水塘上的枯樹

城堡棚架高高立於護城河
水塘上的枯樹
每個早上，鳥上枝頭，枯樹盛放。

可能只是三隻棲居的
鸕鶿，脖子猶如火槍擊錘，還有
一隻像臨床醫師的琵鷺，撅起長啄；

黃昏的鷺，牠們的腳纖幼得
無法落地；珍珠粉紅鳳頭鸚鵡列陣
猶如聯邦，每一隻都散發自己的光芒，

枯樹或者只是一個煙靄瀰漫的大燭臺
棲停其上的白鷺，輕輕搖曳，直至睡眠聖者——
在燭火中醒來，又僵硬地垂下。

古怪的早晨， 處處血旗
處處軍綠：一枚靜止的榴彈
藏著多少國王鸚鵡。一受驚就炸個粉碎。

鴛鴦甚少出現，牠們的雛鳥
在廊柱間漂浮。日間
喜鵲靠邊，從樹頂跳到嶙峋的岩塔

巨大的布穀鳥扇翅闖來，厲叫
警報，翅膀上的警報沒有亮起。

朝代拼圖完後，這時候高調的

朱鷺游划而去，啄食
幾片牧場。無論多麼青綠，永遠
都是牛皮紙上的水彩。

(宋子江　譯)

The Tin Wash Dish

Lank poverty, dank poverty,
its pants wear through at fork and knee.
It warms its hands over burning shames,
refers to its fate as Them and He
and delights in things by their hard names:
rag and toejam, feed and paw—
don't guts that down, there ain't no more!
Dank poverty, rank poverty,
it hums with a grim fidelity
like wood-rot with a hint of orifice,
wet newspaper jammed in the gaps of artifice,
and disgusts us into fierce loyalty.
It's never the fault of those who love:
poverty comes down from above.
Let it dance chairs and smash the door,
it arises from all that went before
and every outsider's the enemy—
Jesus Christ turned this over with his stick
and knights and philosophers turned it back.
Rank poverty, lank poverty,
chafe in its crotch and sores in its hair,
still a window's clean if it's made of air,
not webby silver like a sleeve.
Watch out if this does well at school
and has to leave and longs to leave:
someone, sometime, will have to pay.
Shave with toilet soap, run to flesh,
astound the nation, rule the army,
still you wait for the day you'll be sent back
where books or toys on the floor are rubbish
and no one's allowed to come and play
because home calls itself a shack
and hot water crinkles in the tin wash dish.

錫洗盤

清瘦的貧窮，陰濕的貧窮，
褲子的腳叉和膝蓋穿了幾個洞。
羞恥之心燒暖了手心，
呼命運為「他們」或「他」
名字粗簡讓他滿足：
碎布、趾泥、飼料、爪子——
別吃了，都沒了！
陰濕的貧窮，階級的貧窮，
貧窮哼著歌，冷峻地盡忠
就像腐木病蝕出零星的洞，
濡濕的報紙塞滿陰謀的縫，
貧窮讓噁心，強烈地進忠。
錯總不在所愛的人身上：
只是貧窮從天而降。
讓貧窮跳椅子舞，砸破大門，
它來自過去累積的種種
每一個外人都是敵人——
耶穌基督用棍子把它挑翻
騎士和哲學家又把它還原。
階層的貧窮，清瘦的貧窮，
大腿內側的擦損，頭髮遮掩的腫痛，
乾淨的是空無一物的窗口，
好過銀飾網綴的袖口。
如果在學校表現良好，那就要小心了，
結局只有離開，甚至渴望離開：
某人某刻總要付出代價。
用廁皂剃鬚，越發虛胖，
震驚家國，統率三軍，
你仍然等著自己被遣返的一天
地板上的書籍和玩具都是垃圾
不許任何人來玩
因為家自稱陋棚
熱水在錫洗盤裏泛著漣漪。

(宋子江　譯)

The Farm Terraces

Beautiful merciless work
around slopes of earth
terraces cut by curt hoe
at the orders of hunger
or a pointing lord.
Levels eyed up to rhyme
copied from grazing animals
round the steeps of earth,
balconies filtering water
down stage to stage of drop.
Wind-stirred colours of crop
swell between walked bunds
miles of grass-rimmed contour
harvests down from the top
by hands long in the earth.
Baskets of rich made soil
boosted up poor by the poor,
ladder by freestone prop
stanzas of chant-long lines
by backwrenching slog, before
money, gave food and drunk
but rip now like slatted sails
(some always did damn do)
down the abrupts of earth.

梯田

漂亮而殘忍的傑作
在傾斜的土坡上
短鋤頭掘出梯田
下命令的是飢餓
還是指指戳戳的地主
層層向尾韻看齊
模仿吃著草的動物
在傾斜的土坡上
露臺過濾掉的水
從舞臺流落水滴的舞臺
莊稼有被風翻起的顏色
在海邊馬路之間膨脹
草圍起數英里長的輪廓
在土地上，躬身臂長
從最高的梯田收割下來
籃子裏都是人造沃壤
攀比誰比誰更窮
砂岩撐起一把梯
詩節的詩行長如聖頌
幹斷背脊的苦活，金錢
未賺到，便吃喝揮霍
但是撕開來像頁帆片片
（總有人幹下去）
落入土地的深淵。

(宋子江　譯)

費平樂，1960 年生於里斯本，為醫科畢業生，其後研究當代語言文學並取得博士學位。現為里斯本大學文學院文學教授，並主理葡萄牙教育部「國家閱讀計劃」。他出版過六本詩集、兩本散文和兩本小說，另譯有葡文版波德賴爾的《惡之花》、魏倫的《憂鬱詩篇》及博爾赫斯的所有詩作。

Fernando Pinto do Amaral, writer, poet, literary critic and translator, was born in Lisbon in 1960. He is a professor at the University of Lisbon, where he has been teaching since 1987. He is currently in charge of the National Reading Plan (Ministry of Education) of Portugal. Amaral's publications include six books of poetry, two books of essays, two volumes of fiction, and two books for children. He has translated into Portuguese Baudelaire's *Les Fleurs du Mal*, Verlaine's *Poèmes Saturniens* and the complete poetical works of Jorge Luis Borges.

費平樂

FERNANDO PINTO DO AMARAL

Insónia

Sair enfim daqui   Ficar enfim
sem coração
sem voz
sem esperar que alguém te venha repetir
suaves melopeias
palavras impossíveis e contudo
sempre tão maviosas como o «amor»
ou a «eternidade» ou sobretudo
a «poesia»   Não há
nunca houve razões para falar
canções para embalar todas as noites
a tua insónia

無眠

終於離開這裏，終於
沒有了心
沒有了聲音
也不再等人向你重複
柔和的旋律
不可能的詞語，雖然
它們總是那般溫柔，一如「愛」
「永恆」，尤其是「詩」。
沒有理由，也不曾有過理由
淺唱著搖籃曲，哄你的無眠入睡

(姚風　譯)

Insomnia

To get out of here at last   To be at last
without heart
without voice
without hope that someone will come to repeat
for you gentle melopeias
words impossible and at the same time
always so sweet like "love"
or "eternity" or most of all
"poetry"   There are
no reasons nor ever were to murmur
lullabies to gently rock to sleep each night
your insomnia

(Translated by Alexis Levitin)

Farmacolgia

the sobs of life itself
—Marilyn Monroe

Era depois da morte Norma Jeane
foi há cinquenta anos e é agora
Continuas aqui vejo-te ainda
sozinha nesse quarto procurando
uma saída para tanto medo
desde sempre contigo—«terror beyond fear»
Era só isso—medo—o que sentias
diante dos fotógrafos   das câmaras
o que sentes agora nessa casa
ou no jardim enquanto todos dormem
e ficas acordada toda a noite
ao som do vento que te embala a insónia
à espera de uma porta que se abra
de alguém que ainda te ame   que te escute
que leia o que tu escreves   frases curtas
com o pânico lá dentro   Talvez queiras
esconder-te algures onde ninguém te veja
dormir   escapar   fugir mais uma vez
de todos   de ti mesma   dos abutres
que te seguem   perseguem   que te sugam
o sangue e a beleza e o talento
em nome do showbiz   Deves saber
que estão fora de moda os barbitúricos
e já não se usa hidrato de cloral
Agora cada dia tomarias
coisas mais evoluídas   mais suaves
benzodiazepinas ou prozac
e se todo o infinito for apenas
questão de bioquímica talvez
também eu te aconselhe como o outro
Toma os teus comprimidos rapariga
toma comprimidos
Olha que não há mais metafísica no mundo senão comprimidos
Olha que as religiões e as filosofias
não nos ensinam mais que a farmacologia
Mas acima de tudo não te assustes
prometo que não vais ficar sozinha
Brentwood fica tão perto de Lisboa
e hei-de ir ter contigo onde estiveres
Peço-te apenas que não tenhas medo
e se quiseres uma destas noites
agarra no telefone e fala-me em silêncio
Sabes que estou aqui
para te ouvir   para te dizer «shhh»
para chorar de novo com as tuas lágrimas
até adormeceres

藥物學

生活本身的嗚咽

—— 瑪麗蓮 · 夢露

諾瑪 · 珍妮去世五十年後
你還在這裏，我見到你仍舊
獨自在這個房間，為如此多的恐懼
尋找出口，它始終伴隨著你——「恐怖超越恐懼」
就是它——恐懼——你曾在
攝影師的鏡頭前所感覺的
和你此時在這所房子裏或者花園裏所感覺的一樣
眾人都在酣睡，只有你輾轉難眠
任風聲搖盪你的不眠之夜
你在等待一扇門，被一個愛你的人打開
聽你傾訴，或者讀你寫給他的短句，
句子藏著恐懼　也許你也想藏在某個地方
沒有人看到你睡覺　逃離　逃離
所有的人　逃離你自己　逃離追趕你迫害你的禿鷹，
牠們以娛樂業的名義壓榨你的鮮血　美貌　才華
你要知道，服用巴比妥已不流行
也不再使用水合氯醛
時至今日，你應該服用更新更柔和的藥物
比如苯二氮或百憂解
如果無限的問題只是生物化學的問題
或許我也會和別人一樣建議你服用藥物
姑娘，吃藥吧
吞下這些藥片
你看　當今世界除了藥物學已沒有形而上學
你看　宗教和哲學傳授給我們的不過是
藥物學
不過　重要的是你不再害怕，我向你保證
你不會孤獨一人
布倫特伍德離里斯本很近
你無論在甚麼地方我可以找到你
如果你害怕　在這樣的一個夜晚
你可以打電話給我　在寂靜中向我訴說
你知道我在這裏
為了聽你傾訴，為了對你說「噓！」
為了讓你用你的眼淚再哭一次
直到睡去

(姚風　譯)

Pharmacology

the sobs of life itself
—Marilyn Monroe

It was after the death of Norma Jean
fifty years ago and it is now
You are still here I see you still
alone in that room looking for
a way out of all that fear
that was always with you—"terror beyond fear"
It was just that—fear—that you felt
facing the photographers   the cameras
what you feel now in this house
or in the garden while everyone's asleep
and you lie awake all night
beneath the sound of the wind that rocks your insomnia
waiting for a door to open
on someone who still loves you   listens to you
reads what you write   short phrases
with the panic inside   Maybe you want
to hide somewhere where no one can see you
to sleep   escape   flee once again
from everyone   from yourself   from the vultures
that follow you in pursuit   that suck
your blood and beauty and talent
in the name of showbiz   You must know
that barbiturates are out of style
and that no one uses chloral hydrate anymore
Now every day you would take
more advanced products   gentler ones
Benzodiazpines or Prozac
and if all infinity were just
a question of biochemistry perhaps
I too would advise you as the other did
Take your pills, little girl,
take your pills
See how there's no metaphysics in the world except for pills
See how religion and philosophy
teach us nothing more than pharmacology
But above all don't get scared
I promise you won't be alone
Brentwood is so close to Lisbon
and I will come to be with you wherever you are
I only ask you not to be afraid
and if you want one of these nights
to grab the phone and speak to me in silence

you know that I am here
to listen to you   to say "shhhh"
to cry once more your tears
until you fall asleep

(Translated by Alexis Levitin)

Escotoma

Não sei o que é um espírito. Ninguém
conhece a fundo a luz do seu abismo
enquanto o vento à noite vai abrindo
as infinitas portas de uma casa
vazia. A minha voz
procura responder a outra voz,
ao choro dos espectros que celebram
a sua missa negra, o seu eterno
sobressalto. Num ermo
da cidade magoada escuto ainda
o rumor de um oráculo,
a febre de um adeus que se prolonga
no estertor dos ponteiros de um relógio,
nesse ritmo feroz, na pulsação
do meu sangue exilado que recorda
um abrigo divino. Pai nosso, que estás
entre o céu e a terra, conduz-me
ao precipício onde hibernou a alma
e ensina-me a romper a madrugada
como se a minha face fosse
um estilhaço da tua
e nela derretessem, por milagre,
estas gotas de gelo ou de cristal
que não sabem ser lágrimas.

暗點

我不知道甚麼是精神。人們對其
深淵的光芒一無所知，而風會打開
一所空房子所有無盡的門。
我的聲音極力回答另一個聲音，
伴隨幽靈的哭泣，他們在舉行
黑色的彌撒，這
永遠的惶恐。在被踐踏的城市廢墟上
我依舊聽到
一個預言者的胡言亂語
神祇的狂熱，以兇猛的節奏
撥動鐘錶的指針，
激蕩我被放逐的血液，
令我想起神的庇護。聖父，你存於
天地之間，引我至靈魂在此冬眠
的懸崖，教我如何打破黎明
彷若我的臉頰是
你的臉頰的一塊碎片
水珠或水晶從臉頰
奇蹟般地滴落
但不知道變成眼淚。

(姚風　譯)

Scotoma

I don't know what a spirit is. No one
knows in depth the light of his own abyss
as at night the wind opens
the infinite doors of an empty
house, one by one. My voice
tries to respond to another voice,
to the lament of ghosts celebrating
their black mass, their eternal
disquiet. In a forgotten place
of the damaged city I listen still
to an oracle's whisper,
to the feverish farewell prolonged
by the dying rattle of the clock's hands,
their ferocious rhythm, the pulsing
of my exiled blood remembering
a divine shelter. Our father who art
between heaven and earth, take me
to the precipice where my soul wintered
and teach me how to burst through the dawn
as if my face were
shrapnel from your face
that would miraculously melt
these crystal icicles
unable to be tears.

(Translated by Ana Hudson)

Cardiologia

Talvez na sua vida o maior estímulo
fosse a curiosidade.

Era o motor de tudo: aproximava-se
de todas as mulheres que conhecia,
mas só lhe interessavam os seus corações.

Cultivava com método essa obsessão
e tal como as crianças costumam fazer
aos brinquedos preferidos,
também ele queria vê-los por dentro,
saber ao certo como funcionavam,
desfibrar lentamente cada esperança,
dissecar com um rigor quase científico
cada angústia ou desejo inconfessável
até saborear o gosto sempre novo
de cada uma dessas células.

Após cada experiência, observava
aqueles corações já desmontados
e, por não conseguir juntar as peças,
guardava-as uma a uma no seu peito.
Era um lugar seguro
e com tantos pedaços de outras vidas
na sua pulsação descompassada
podia enfim acreditar
que tinha também ele um coração.

心學

也許，支撐他生命最大的動力
是好奇心。

那是一切動力之源：接近
所有他認識的女子，
但只想俘獲她們的芳心。

就像小孩子對待
心愛的玩具，
緊隨這心癮，
他還想窺探內裏乾坤，
確切知道它如何運作，
慢慢剝開層層希望，
以近似科學的精確，
解剖苦痛或者隱秘的希冀
直至品嚐
每一個細胞的鮮活。

每次經歷後，他都看到
那被拆解的心
無法還原，
於是他把所有的零件藏於胸中。
這才是安全的地方，
而且有這麼多他人生命的碎片
在他的心脈中瘋狂搏動，

他終於確信，
他自己也有一顆心。

(姚風　譯)

Cardiology

The greatest motivation in his life
was perhaps curiosity.

It drove him on: he approached
every woman he met,
but he was only interested in their hearts.

He methodically followed this obsession
and like a child
with his favourite toy
he also wanted to see what was inside,
find out exactly how it worked,
to shred each hope in slow motion,
dissect with almost scientific rigour
each anguish, each unavowable desire,
till he felt the ever fresh taste
in each one of those cells.

After each experiment, he observed
the dismantled hearts
and, not being able to reassemble them,
he gathered them one by one into his breast.
It was a safe place
and holding so many pieces of other lives
pulsating out of step
he could at last believe
that he also had a heart.

(Translated by Ana Hudson)

格列勃·舒爾比亞科夫，生於1971年，畢業於莫斯科國立大學新聞學系，現居莫斯科。他的第一部詩集《彈指》（2001）獲得「勝利詩歌獎」。他也曾出版過遊記隨筆《格拉巴酒人》（2002）和《叔叔的夢》（2005），小說《希南之書》（2005）、《海嘯》（2008）和《非斯》（2010）。他創作的戲劇《普希金在美國》贏得「2005劇中人」大獎。他已把泰德·休斯、羅拔·哈斯的詩，以及威斯坦·休·奧登的散文翻譯成俄文。他的第二本詩集《橡實》出版於2007年，詩集《防火箱》入選2012年「最佳翻譯書籍獎」候選名單。他最近出版的詩集是《給雅庫布的信》（2012，英譯版2014），目前正在寫下一本詩集《打字機上的詩》。

Gleb Shulpyakov, born in 1971, graduated from Moscow State University with a degree in journalism, and lives in Moscow. His first poetry collection *The Flick* (2001) was awarded the prestigious Triumph Prize. His second book of poems, *Acorn*, was published in 2007. Shulpyakov has published travel essays, *Persona Grappa* (2002) and *Uncle's Dream* (2005), the novels *The Sinan Book* (2005), *Tsunami* (2008), and *Fez* (2010) and numerous essays and criticism for Russian periodicals. His play *Pushkin in America* was laureate of "Dramatis personae" concourse in 2005. He translated the poetry of Ted Hughes and Robert Hass, and W. H. Auden's essays into Russian. The poetry collection *A Fireproof Box* (Canarium Books, 2011) translated into English by Christopher Mattison, was shortlisted for the 2012 Best Translated Book Award. The English translation of *Letters to Yakub* (2012) was published by Canarium Books in 2014. He is currently working on the collection *Poems on a Typewriter*.

格列勃 · 舒爾比亞科夫

GLEB SHULPYAKOV

ворона прыгает с одной
тяжелой ветки на другую—
здесь что-то кончилось со мной,
а я живу и в ус не дую,
небытия сухой снежок
еще сдувая вместо пыли
—так по ночам стучит движок,
который вырубить забыли

烏鴉從一根
沉重的樹枝跳到另一根——
這裏有甚麼事物與我完結了，
而我活著，不吹鬍子，
虛無的乾冷的雪花
還在代替灰塵吹著
——就這樣每夜滑板敲擊作響，
人們忘記了把它砍光

（晴朗李寒　譯）

a crow leaps from one
heaving branch to another—
something ended here with me,
yet I go on living, not really caring,
the dry snow of nonexistence,
me blowing like dust
—at night, a sputtering engine
they forgot to cut down

(Translated by Christopher Mattison)

поэзия растет из ничего—
возьмем картину, что
висит против окна
—точнее, момент, когда
на стене появляется тень
от дерева, что растет
за окном—

картина неизменна, хотя
нарисованная река
течет—а тени, наоборот,
то видны, то нет
(в зависимости от облаков)
и мало-помалу
наползают на реку

неподвижна одна
стена, но поскольку она
никому не видна,
(с тем, что на ней)—стихи
о движении / покое,
объекте / субъекте,
искусстве и жизни
(не говоря об окне)

так и останутся не-
написанными

詩歌生長於虛無——
設想有一幅畫，它
懸掛在窗子對面的牆上
——準確說，當時
牆壁上出現了一棵樹的
陰影，它就生長在
窗子外面——

圖畫不會改變，儘管
畫著的河水
在流動——而陰影，相反，
時隱，時現
（取決於那些雲朵）
它們一點一點
在河面上爬行

只有牆
一動不動，但是不一定
誰也看不到它，
（因為是在它的上面）——詩歌
是關於運動／靜止，
客體／主體，
藝術與生活
（別提到窗子）
就這樣留給那些
沒有寫到的事物

(晴朗李寒　譯)

poetry grows from nothing—
like a picture
facing a window,
or rather, the moment
shadows appear on the wall
of trees growing
beyond the window—

the canvas remains untouched,
though the sketched river
flows—and the shadows, in contrast,
appear and fade
(depending on the clouds)
floating bit by bit
along the river

a wall is a single fixed
thing, but because
no one sees it
(and what's upon it)—a poem
in motion / rest,
object / subject,
art and life
(not to mention the window)
remains un-
written

(Translated by Christopher Mattison)

Армянский Триптих

1
арарат—
шапку твою из рукава достану,
на брови надвину—
никто не заметит

2
выйду на лестницу—
первая травой заросла, вторая из камня,
а на третьей снег не сошёл
—ереван мой

3
берег есть, а воды нет
храм на берегу есть—берега нет
небо над храмом есть, храма нет
отдай, что взял—севан!

亞美尼亞[1] 三章

1
亞拉拉特[2]——
我從袖口探手夠到你的帽子，
拉至眉毛上——
誰也不能發現

2
我走上階梯——
第一個雜草叢生，第二個石頭所建，
而第三個雪沒化盡
——我的葉里溫[3]

3
有岸，無水
岸上有寺院——無岸
寺院上空有天——無寺院
請把拿走的，還給我吧，——塞凡[4]！

（晴朗李寒　譯）

Armenian Triptych

1

ararat—
I pull down your cap
from a sleeve donning dark
brows so no one will see—

2

go out on the stairs—
the first overgrown in grass, the second stone,
and snow upon the third
—my Yerevan

3

there is a shore, but no water
a cathedral on the shore, but no shore
sky above the cathedral, but no cathedral,
return what's been taken—sevan!

(Translated by Christopher Mattison)

譯註：

1. 亞美尼亞共和國是一個位於歐亞交界高加索地區的國家，也是在蘇聯解體之後獨立的眾多共和國之一。
2. 亞拉拉特山 (Mount Ararat，阿拉臘山) 俯瞰著亞美尼亞的首都，同時也是該國之精神象徵，《創世記》一書中記載，諾亞方舟在大洪水後，最後停泊的地方就在亞拉拉特山上。
3. 葉里溫 (Yerevan)，是亞美尼亞共和國的首都和經濟、文化中心，外高加索古城之一。
4. 塞凡湖是高加索最大的高山湖泊。離葉里溫六十公里，是著名遊覽勝地。

Прадо

Мясные ряды Рубенса.
Битая птица Гойи, перья испачканы грязью.
Креветки Босха, требуха Брейгеля—
кипят, бурлят в огромных чанах.
Вяленая рыба Эль Греко.
Между прилавков снуют карлы, буффоны.
«Педро Ивановиц Потемкин» в меховой шапке.
Крики, конский топот, лязг металла—
все сливается в один базарный грохот.
Только в полотняных рядах Рафаэля тихо—
ветер играет голубым отрезом.
И снова стук, скрежет, брань.
Отрубленное ухо кровоточит на пол.
«Взяли, поднимаем!»—кричит кто-то простуженным голосом.
В небе медленно вырастает силуэт креста.
Всё замирает.
В эту бесконечную секунду тишины
слышно как в пещере потрескивает огонь.
Плеск весла на переправе.
Шелест инкунабулы Иеронима
и стук прялки.

... На следующий день мы проснулись рано
и целовались в постели, не размыкая веки,
как летучие мыши. Два рисунка
—два наброска на холсте Мадрида.
Картина, которую никто никогда не увидит.

普拉多[1]

魯本斯的一排排肉案。
戈雅打碎的鳥，羽毛粘滿血污。
博斯[2]的小蝦，勃魯蓋爾的內臟——
在巨大的桶裏沸騰，翻滾。
埃爾·格列柯[3]的乾巴魚。
侏儒和小丑在櫃檯間往來穿梭。
「佩德羅·伊萬諾維茨·波將基」[4]戴著皮帽子。
人聲喧噪，馬蹄雜遝，金屬叮噹——
一切都攪拌進一個集市的轟鳴聲中。
只有在拉斐爾的亞麻布攤上一片安靜——
微風像藍色的布料吹拂。
又是敲打聲，摩擦聲，吵罵聲。
割掉的耳朵在地上流著血。
「抓住了，抬起來！」有人用感冒的嗓音叫嚷。
天空中緩緩出現十字架的剪影。
一切都沉寂。
在這無限的寂靜的一秒鐘裏
聽得見火焰在山洞中劈啪作響。
渡口上船槳的擊水聲。
希羅尼穆斯的古版書窸窸窣窣，
紡車吱呀。

第二天我們早早醒來
眼皮沒睜開，就在被窩裏親吻，
像蝙蝠。像兩張畫
——馬德里油畫布上的兩張草圖。
這畫面，任何人從來都沒見過。

（晴朗李寒　譯）

譯註：

1. 普拉多博物館（Prado），建於十八世紀，位於馬德里，被認為是世界上最偉大的博物館之一，亦是收藏西班牙繪畫作品最全面、最權威的美術館。
2. 希羅尼穆斯·博斯（Hieronymus Bosch ，1450–1516），荷蘭畫家。他富有想像力的畫作充滿了荒唐的形式和怪異的象徵主義。
3. 埃爾·格列柯（El Greco, 1541–1614，「希臘人」）出生於希臘的克里特島，原名多明尼克斯·希奧托科普羅斯，是西班牙文藝復興時期著名的幻想風格主義畫家。
4. 即彼得·伊萬諾維奇·波特金（1617–1700），俄羅斯外交官，軍事領導者。

Prado

Butcher stalls of Rubens.
Goya's beaten birds, feathers daubed in mud.
Bosch's shrimp, Brueghel's entrails—
seething, boiled in enormous vats.
El Greco's dried fish.
Dwarves scurry between the counters, buffoons.
"Pedro Ivanowitz Potemkin" in a fur hat.
Shouting, the clatter of horses, clanging metal—
everything merging in the din of a single bazaar.
Raphael's rows of linen the sole calm—
wind playing in the sky-blue lengths.
And then another thump, gnashing, curses.
A severed ear bleeds onto the floor.
"Hoist it up!"—someone shouts in a gruff voice.
A cross's silhouette emerges in the sky.
                                        Everyone stops.
The sound of a flame crackling in a cave
echoes over this infinite moment of silence.
The splashing of oars fording a river.
Hieronymus's rustling incunabula
and the rumble of spinning wheels.

... We woke early the next day,
kissed in bed, not opening our eyes,
like bats. Two drawings,
two sketches on the canvas of Madrid.
A painting no one will see.

(Translated by Christopher Mattison)

качается домик
на белой воде
бульварного неба—
а, может, нигде
—качается
между бульваров
москва *(давно*
опустели москвы
рукава)—одна
по привычке
дворняга нужду
справляет в ее
позабытом углу
(мелькает как облако
жизнь в голове)
—и дальше бежит
по небесной
москве

小房子搖晃
在街心花園
白色的水面上——
啊，也許，沒這個地方
——它搖晃
在街心花園之間
莫斯科*（莫斯科的*
河叉早就
空了）——一條
看家狗習慣地
在牠被遺忘的角落
撒尿
（生活如同雲朵
在頭腦中閃爍）
——牠繼續向前跑去
沿著令人神往的
莫斯科

(晴朗李寒　譯)

a cottage swaying
on the white water
of a dime store heaven—
or maybe nowhere
—swaying
between moscow's
boulevards *(moscow's
sleeves emptied
long ago)*—a single
mongrel, by force
of habit, must
celebrate in a
forgotten corner
*(yes, an entire life
flashing like a cloud)*
—dashes further
through celestial
Moscow

(Translated by Christopher Mattison)

—n.a.

наших мертвецов
продрогшие виолончели
мы вынимаем из футляров
и день за днем, нота за нотой—
трогая слабые, сухие струны
—вспоминаем, как они звучали

—— 致 *n.a.*

從匣子裏
我們取出我們亡者的
顫抖的大提琴
一日復一日，音符連音符——
撫摸著鬆弛乾澀的琴弦
——我們回想起，它們從前的演奏

(晴朗李寒　譯)

—*p.a.*

our dead's
frozen cellos
pulled from cases—
day after day, note for note,
weak plucking, dry strings
—we recall their sounds

(Translated by Christopher Mattison)

宋琳，1959 年生於福建廈門，祖籍寧德。1983 年畢業於上海華東師範大學中文系。1991 年移居法國，曾就讀於巴黎第七大學遠東系，先後在新加坡、阿根廷居留。2003 年以來受聘於國內幾所大學執教，目前專事寫作與繪畫。著有詩集《城市人》（1987）、《門廳》（2000）、《斷片與驪歌》（2006）、《城牆與落日》（2007）、《雪夜訪戴》（2015）、《口信》（2015）；隨筆集《對移動冰川的不斷接近》（2014）、《俄爾甫斯回頭》（2014）；編有詩選《空白練習曲》（2002）。現任《今天》文學雜誌的詩歌編輯 、《讀詩》主編之一及《當代國際詩壇》編委。宋琳曾獲得「鹿特丹國際詩歌節獎」、「上海文學獎」、「東蕩子詩歌獎」等。

Song Lin was born in Xiamen, Fujian in 1959. He graduated from East China Normal University in Shanghai in 1983 and in 1991 moved to France to pursue graduate work in Far Eastern Studies at Université Paris Diderot. He has since lived in Singapore and Argentina, taught at various universities in China from 2003, and currently writes and paints full-time. His poetry collections include *City Dwellers* (1987), *Vestibule* (2000), *Fragments and Farewell Songs* (2006), *The City Wall and the Setting Sun* (2007), *Visiting Mr. Dai on Snowy Nights* (2015), and *Oral Message* (2015). His essay collections include *Continuous Approaches to Moving Icebergs* (2014) and *Orpheus Looks Back* (2014). With the poet Zhang Zao, he edited the anthology *Blank Etudes* (2002). He is an editor for the journals *Today* and *Reading Poetry*, and serves on the editorial board of *Contemporary International Poetry*. He is a recipient of the Rotterdam International Poetry Award, the Shanghai Literature Award, and the Dong Dangzi Poetry Award.

宋琳

SONG LIN

選自〈脈水歌〉
——重讀《水經注》

1

大河在遠方閃爍，猶如一道
來自北極的光。太陽的火舌下
羿的箭矢穿過雲的旗幡
我移動，像《山海經》中的測量員
雁陣在藍天書寫一個人字
流水浣洗著林壑的耳朵
在我的衣襟前製造一個節日
飛瀑在懸崖絕壁激起回響
一條又一條河穿過我的軀體
帝國的通都和采邑中有我的驛站
美人因遲暮而憂傷，醒來
衣袖空留昨夜的餘溫

2

岸草青蔥尾隨我遠去
而生活本是在岸上築居
為甚麼要告別笙歌和畫舫
去追逐蠻荒的河流？
為甚麼騎驢，飲風，偃蹇而進
易水而弱水，塞北又江南？
漫長的行旅中，孤獨已變成
心的刺客。夜半客船上
家書的爐炭烘暖我的雙手
出發的日子，話別的時刻而今安在？
兇年又加上不馴服的河道
星星的沙粒壅塞平原

4

倘若青鳥來過，曾棲於甚麼枝頭？
羅盤搜尋到哪一座仙島或靈山？
裸國殘缺，怪物的想像同樣殘缺
龍族的血液裏有牠們的低語、尖叫
〈禹貢〉山水猶在，貢船早傾覆
接著走來了遊俠，縱橫家
和篡位者儀仗中大象雄武的步伐
這片土地的傳説，河流的傳説
像炭黑的赤壁被燒得滾燙
像石上的勒文，只有風能夠識讀
連同智者的浩嘆都將化為烏有
影子交錯，有誰曾抵達過彼岸？

5

漁父調舟而去，桂棹輕點
拋下一支惱人的〈滄浪歌〉
多事之秋的高樹用傷疤的瞎眼眺望
我走過的泥足深陷的路
一隻蝴蝶被塵土壓住有無原由？

一隻螢火蟲為我照明是否出於自願？
除了繼續早已開始的仰觀俯察
涇屬渭汭的清濁，南北分流的盤根錯節
現在豈不是一一稽考的時候？
説，即便最終等於不説
像流星的湮滅，石棺的沉默
鐵函有朝一日會浮出深井

7

開創的人物，天之驕子
遙遠如來自某個河外星系
沿著傾斜的日影下凡
敷土，祭奠高山，命名了百川
那傳説中的水王不曾回來
廣漠掩埋遲到者的悲哀
河與人喧響兩種孤寂
一如那不可能停下的箭矢
唯有脈跳還在呼應地下的湧動
唯有記憶匯合成更遼闊的河
當我躊躇著不知該向何處去
月亮那水的魂魄引導我

8

經典已撲散。在扭曲的時代
我只想做一個脈水人
在精心繪製的地圖上規劃
一度是桃花源，後來是戰場的山水
渴時我就以朝聖者的姿勢彎下腰
風像色情的山鬼挑逗我：
看啊，一切皆流。但重泉中
我的影子卻如如不動
變化多端的四季的儀表
漲落的水文，讓我徒然興嘆
並連連發問：甚麼樣的鉤沉索隱
可以追回遁走的暗流？

10

急迫的鷹唳叫著，唳叫著，唳叫著
大地之鷹，展翅在雲端
那聲音像黃昏天空的一個亮點
神秘的河圖的一個疑點
像從殷墟飛來的傳奇的巫祝
戴著面具，發出預言：
「旅者，你該向視域外搜尋
在傾聽中配製魔咒的力量
你也該知道源頭的涓滴原本弱小
逆流而上即與那一脈活水為鄰
夢想的顛躓也是生活的顛躓
當大河上的彩虹橫絕遠空」

Selections from "Song of Exploring the Waterways"

—Rereading the *Commentary on the Water Classic*

1

The great river glistens in the distance
like an aurora. Yi's arrows pass cloud banners
under the sun's flamed tongue.
I move like a surveyor in the *Classic of Mountains and Seas*.
A formation of geese writes the ideogram for person in the blue sky
flowing water washes the ears of the forest ravine
and creates a holiday on the front of my silk robes.
The flying waterfall echoes over the sheer cliffs.
River after river passes by my body.
There are hitching posts for me in imperial Tongdu and Caiyi
The beauty mourns her faded youth, and when she awakens,
all that's left is last night's warmth in her sleeves.

2

Riverbank grasses and greenery follow me into the distance
yet life builds its home on the riverbank.
Why do we leave behind flute songs and pleasure boats
to chase the savage river?
Why ride a donkey, drink the wind, grow weary and enter
the Yi or Ruo Rivers, Sai Bei or Jiangnan?
On a long journey, loneliness becomes
the heart's assassin. At midnight on the passenger ship
the charcoal of letters from home warms my hands.
The day of departure, the moment of farewell, and where am I now?
Famine years and untamed rivers,
star sands congest the plains.

4

If the black messenger bird came, on which branch did it alight?
Which Immortal Island or Soul Mountain did the compass find?
When Naked Country is battered, monsters' imaginations are also battered
the dragon people's blood holds their whispers and screams
The mountains and rivers in *Yu Gong* still remain, but the boats with imperial
  offerings sank long ago
Then come the knights-errant, the strategists
and the bold elephant-like march of the usurpers
The myths of this land, the myths of this river
like the coal black Red Cliffs being burned
like engravings in stone only the wind can read.
Together with the deep sighs of sages, they will all become nothingness.
Shadows intertwine, yet who has been to the other shore?

5

The fisherman turns his boat around and departs, gently dipping the cassia oars
casting off an annoying Song of the Cang Lang River
A tall tree in a troubled autumn looks over the scene with eyes of scars.
The road I walked where my feet sunk deep in the mud.
Was a butterfly crushed in the dust for no reason?

Does the firefly shine for me of its own will?
In addition to surveying the clear and muddy bend
where the Jing and Wei Rivers converge,
the complications of which flow north or south
how is now not the time to inspect them all one by one?
To speak, in the end, is the same as not speaking,
like a meteor's annihilation, the silence of the sarcophagus.
One day the metal letter will float up from the well.

7

The first human, the pride of heaven,
distant as if from another galaxy,
descended to this earth along the slanted sun shadow,
laying out soil, offering sacrifices on the mountain, and naming the
hundred rivers
That mythic king of the waters has never returned.
Vastness buries the sorrow of those who came late.
Rivers and people resound with two kinds of loneliness
like the unstoppable arrow
only arteries echo underground surges,
only memories converge into wider rivers.
When I hesitate and don't know where to go
the moon, that water spirit, guides me.

8

The Classics have been altered. In a twisted age
I just want to be an explorer,
to plan on a meticulous map.
Once there was the Peach Blossom Land, then a battlefield terrain
thirsty I'll bend forward in a pilgrim's posture
and the wind will titillate me like an erotic mountain ghost.
Look, everything is flowing, but in the layers of the spring water,
my reflection seems motionless.
The appearance of the ever-changing seasons,
the fluctuating hydrology makes me gasp in vain with joy.
I ask again and again: what sort of lost references
can bring back the fleeting undercurrents?

10

The urgent eagle is calling, calling, calling.
The eagle of the earth spreads its wings in the clouds.
The sound is a bright spot in the dusk sky,
a dubious spot on the mysterious river chart
like the legendary shaman who flew from the Ruins of Yin
wearing a mask, offering a prophecy:
"Travelers, you should search beyond vision
and create the power of magic in listening
You should know the stream that comes from the source is weak at first,
but if you walk upstream, you'll get close to the flowing water.
Stumbles in dreams are stumbles in life
when the rainbow over the river cuts across the distant sky."

(Translated by Jami Proctor Xu)

多和田葉子，用日、德雙語寫作的小說家和詩人，1960 年生於東京。1982 年移居德國，後來在蘇黎世大學獲得德國文學博士。1993 年以短篇小說《倒插門的狗女婿》獲芥川獎，她1996 年獲德國「沙米索文學獎」，並在2005 年獲德意志聯邦共和國歌德勳章。英譯的小說包括《倒插門的狗女婿》(1998)、《歐陸開始的地方》(2002)、《面對橋樑》(2007)、《裸眼》(2009) 等。

Yoko Tawada was born in Tokyo in 1960. She was educated at Waseda University and has lived in Germany since 1982. She received her Ph.D. in German literature from the University of Zurich. She writes in both German and Japanese and was awarded the prestigious Akutagawa Prize in 1993 for her short story *The Bridegroom Was a Dog*. In 1996, she won the Adelbert von Chamisso Prize. In 2005, she was awarded the Goethe Medal, an official decoration of the Federal Republic of Germany. English translations of her fiction include *The Bridegroom Was a Dog* (Kodansha International, 1998), *Where Europe Begins* (New Directions, 2002), *Facing the Bridge* (New Directions, 2007), and *The Naked Eye* (New Directions, 2009).

多和田葉子

YOKO TAWADA

線から生まれた人々

4. 米

茶碗いっぱいに星が盛りつけてある
とがった光の先端が
米食う人の舌を甘く刺すと
眼球の裏側にさわやかな風が流れこむ
さっきまで壁のよごれだと思っていたのは七匹の蚊その脚にはえた産毛まではっきり見える
星米を食べると遠くが見えるのだそうだ
三十キロ先の海辺で幼な児が鼻血をたらしながら蟹と遊んでいるのが見える
三年先に無人銀行の窓が風にあおられてバタンバタンと開いたり閉まったりしているのが見える

7. 太

夜明けと夕闇が溶け合い
暑さと寒さが同じ意味になる時代が来る
ゆっくり歩くと駅は近く感じられ
おせんべいを一枚食べただけでもう満腹で
もう書くのはやめようと思った詩がいつの間にか紙の上に姿を現す

9. 末

袖の末には繊細な手がある
裾の末にはしなやかで力強い足首がある
思考の末には呼吸がある
わたしは
片足を鶴のようにもちあげ
扇を持った右手を翼のように開いて
人から鳥へ
鳥から文字へと変化していく

選自〈自線而生的人們〉

4. 米

盛上滿滿一碗星星
尖銳的光線頭部
溫柔地刺向食米者的舌頭
眼球內部清爽的風流動
剛剛還以為是牆上的污垢，現在連那七隻蚊子腳上長出的細毛
　　都能看清
好像吃了星米就能看清遠方
看得見三十公里外的海邊，淌著鼻血的小孩捉蟹玩兒
看得見三年前無人的銀行之窗被風吹得咣噹咣噹時開時合

7. 太

黎明與黃昏融合在一起
酷暑與寒冷變成同一個意思的時代到來
慢慢走會感覺車站很近
只吃一塊脆餅就已很飽
已決定不再寫的詩卻不覺間出現在紙上

9. 末

袖口的末端有纖細的手
褲管的末端有敏捷且有力的腳踝
思考的末端有呼吸
我像單腳站立的鶴，用手舉起
像握著扇子的右手展開翅膀
從人到鳥
從鳥到文字的演變

（田原、毛乙馨　譯）

Selections from "People Born of Lines"

4. Rice (米)

A pile of stars fills her bowl
The tips of the sharp ray of light
Sweetly sting the mouth of the ones who eat it
A refreshing breeze flows in behind their eyes
What looked like spot on the wall is now seven mosquitoes, the hair of their legs clearly visible
They say eating star-rice allows one to see into the distance
Thirty kilometers away, a small child is visible, nose bleeding, as it plays with a crab
Three years away, the window of an unmanned bank is visible as it blows in the wind, banging open and shut

7. Thick (太)

A time will come when dawn will melt into dusk
Warmth will mean the same as cold
Walk slowly and the station will feel nearer
A single cracker will fill our stomachs
And at the moment one wants to stop writing, a poem appears on the page

9. End (末)

At the end of the sleeve is a sensitive hand
At the end of the hem is a delicate yet strong ankle
At the end of thought is breath
I raise one foot
Like a crane
I spread out my right hand holding a fan
Like a wing
And I transform from human into a bird
From bird to a letter

(Translated by Jeffrey Angels)

Der Hafenpilz

Lachsforellen
die sich unter der Brücke versammeln
um das Feuerwerk
zu erblicken
Ich habe keine Augen
sagt die eine
Bei mir wächst ein Blumenkohl aus dem Kopf
sagt eine andere und
spannt im Wasser ihren Regenschirm auf
(Am Himmel brennen sie Blumen zu Kohle)
Bald fangen die Feuerblätter an
tief im Bierglas zu tanzen
Dann ist es zu spät
Die Lachsforellen schwimmen zurück in die Konservenfabrik
ohne Eintritt zu zahlen

海港蘑菇

鱒魚
在橋下聚集
去看那
煙花盛放
我沒有眼睛
其一說
我認為椰菜花從頭部生長
另一說
並在水裏張開她的傘
（夜空裏已開成荼蘼花事了）
頃刻火樹銀花
舞於啤酒瓶底
為時已晚了
鱒魚回游罐頭工場
無需支付入場費

（方太初　譯）

The Harbor Mushroom

Salmon trout
that assemble under the bridge
to catch a glimpse
of the fireworks
I have no eyes
says one
A cauliflower is growing out of my head
says another and
opens up its umbrella in the water
(On the sky they are burning flowers into coal)
Soon the fire-leaves begin
to dance deep in the beer glass
Then it is too late
the salmon trout swim back
into the canning factory
without paying for entrance

(Translated by Emily Sullivan)

ein gedicht fuer ein Buch

ein wort
ein mord
wenn ich spreche
bin ich nicht da
ein wort
in seinem käfig
fesselnd gefesselt
spuckt einen bericht
über meine taten
über meine karten
kein wort
nur sein schatten
in dem ich ruhe
mein schatten verschwindet darin
nichts wird bewertet
wenn ich schweige
bin ich aus demselben stoff gemacht
wie du
stoffliche zeit
zwischen einem wort
und einem schluck wasser
dort
wo die stimme im fleisch aufwacht
hört man ohne ohren
ein wort
befreit von seinem dienst
ein wort
direkt auf das trommelfell geschrieben
die trommel fällt
lautlos
stimmhaft
ein wort
ein ort

一詩一書

一字
一謀殺案
當我開口
我不在那兒
一字
在其籠裏
迷惑人也被迷惑
吐出報告
我那些往事
我那些卡片
沒有言語
只有其影
我棲息其中
我影消失
無所估算
當我沉默
我乃相同原料所製
一如你
物質時間
在說一字
與啜飲一口水之間
那兒
乃肉體之音醒來之處
你不用耳朵也聽見
一字
自其任務中解脱
一字
直接寫進耳膜內
大鼓倒下
萬籟俱寂
有聲始出
一字
一地

(方太初　譯)

a Poem for a Book

a word
a murder
when i speak
i am not there
a word
in its cage
arresting arrested
spits a report
about my crimes
about my cards
no word
only its shadow
in which i rest
my shadow disappears in it
nothing is judged
when i am silent
i am made of the same material
as you
material time
between one word
and a sip of water
there
where the voice awakes in the flesh
you hear without ears
a word
liberated from its duty
a word
written directly on the eardrum
the drum falls
soundless
voiced
a word
a place

(Translated by Emily Sullivan)

安妮・華曼，集詩人、表演家、教授、編輯、文化活動家於一身，曾任「紐約聖馬克大教堂詩歌計劃」的主任，與艾倫・金斯堡在科羅拉多州納羅帕大學一起創立傑克・凱魯亞克解體詩藝學院。華曼現為納羅帕大學詩學榮譽教授，擔任該校夏季寫作課程的藝術主任。金斯堡常常把華曼稱為「心靈上的妻子」。她曾出版超過40本詩集，包括精微經典系列詩集《快嘴女人》(1974)、《婚姻：審判》(2000)、《海牛／人性》(2009)等。華曼憑藉《暖葦絲三部曲：隱蔽機制的顏色》贏得「2012美國筆會詩歌獎」，2013–2014年獲得「古根漢獎金」，現為美國詩人學院的主席。近幾年，華曼到過日本、印度、中國、摩洛哥、法國、比利時和加拿大等國朗誦她的詩歌。《出版人週報》譽華曼為「反文化巨人」。

Anne Waldman is a poet, performer, professor, editor and cultural activist. She is the former Director of the historic Poetry Project at St Mark's Church in-the-Bowery in New York City, and co-founder with Allen Ginsberg of the Jack Kerouac School of Disembodied Poetics at Naropa University in Boulder, Colorado where she is a Distinguished Professor of Poetics and Artistic Director of The Summer Writing Program. Allen Ginsberg has often referred to Waldman as his "spiritual wife." She is the author of over 40 books of poetry, including the mini-classic *Fast Speaking Woman* (City Lights, 1974), *Marriage: A Sentence* (Penguin Poets, 2000), the book-length hybrid *Manatee/Humanity* (Penguin Poets, 2009), and the feminist epic *The Iovis Trilogy: Colors in the Mechanism of Concealment* (Coffee House, 2011) which is the winner of the 2012 PEN Center USA Award for Poetry. Other recent books include *Gossamurmur* (Penguin Poets, 2013), *Jaguar Harmonics* (Post-Apollo Press, 2014) and the anthology *Cross Worlds: Transcultural Poetics* (Coffee House, 2014), co-edited with Laura Wright. *Voice's Daughter of a Heart Yet To Be Born* is forthcoming from Coffee House Press in 2016. Waldman is the recipient of a Guggenheim Fellowship (2013–14) and a Chancellor of The Academy of American Poets. She has lectured and presented her poetry in Japan, India, China (Wuhan and Beijing), Morocco, France, Belgium, and Canada in recent years. *Publishers Weekly* has deemed Waldman "a counter-cultural giant."

安妮・華曼

ANNE WALDMAN

Hungry Ghost

Hungry Ghost is one of the six realms in the Buddhist Wheel of Life, a place with literal hunger and also insatiable psychological hunger. It symbolizes for me the bottomless appetite for fossil fuel and the destruction of our planet.

Hungry ghost, a morphology all by itself between our realms

Hungry ghost: a restless consciousness eats the world

Sexy ghost, a performer, a demon, a gadfly, a fun-hog

To never have enough be enough get enough to never have enough get
enough be enough

Carbon ghost! Dancing on coals

In a state of mind, unsatisfied, unsettled over what he thinks or she thinks,
what they think what he wants she wants what they want

What the "I" thinks & wants: hieroglyph for the hungry ghost!

Jostled by waves, the real kind, that pull you under
Jostled by fracking, earthquake under your feet
And the earth says don't like it don't do it don't like it hydraulic fracturing
heh heh heh

Turbulent in a shadow realm between waking and sleep

Hungry ghost with sacrifices in the sand, hewn painted characters deep in
the cave, arms and legs that brisk strokes of genius, cinematic animal
gestures running in space, hunting in language, flailing about, writing
with the skeletal stylus of the hungry ghost

Sleeping with the hungry ghost who writes your book of doom

Hungry ghost: a web, a film, a trail, a latent thought set down that won't let
go

The watcher watching you in your hungry ghost fabrication

Gloves off, anything can happen

Hungry ghost, the war machine, sleeping with the humming war machine

Hungry ghost that is a blur between worlds, thrumming on
filaments of desire in a code that summons hallucination of "enemy!
enemy!"

we're the enemy

Enmity of insatiable hunger for oil oil oil!

Threads of desire constantly broken, strings plucked and snapped
Kill for oil

Bleed for oil

the fix is in for the hungry ghost who sings in lamentation

Singing: *To be ghost and so very hungry, the fix is in, the fix is in*

Attachment which is a ghost of yearning,

Yearning for existence, *the fix is in*

Yearning for sustenance, *the fix is in*

Hungry ghosts of the Jurassic, large omnivores startling you with appetite

Hungry ghost ancient in mind, continuity of the mind of all primordial
hungry ghosts

Ravage and ravaging, ravaged and will have ravaged and will ravage and
will have been ravaged the fix is in the fix is in

Hues of glorious white light that pursue you everywhere, spotlight on
desire

Then so bright or fierce you can never rest

How can we ever feed your ravenous hounds?

Or radiant colors of seductive desire, illusive beauty adorn your tattered
frame

Although worn too, transient flickering

Transmigrating through many lifetimes, hungry ghost

Down & dirty on the street, shackled

Body picked over, on a street in a distant street "over there"

Other side of the hungry ghost world

People willing to die there, fighting the hungry ghost

Despots, tyrants, mercenaries, denizens of the hungry ghost world

Stars, atoms, molecules, names family histories, all shackled

The Houghly River right in front of you

Your rivers in lockdown

Ganges in lockdown

Yangtze in lockdown

Bending over into the river of hungry ghost

Torturer can do anything he wants to

Maybe anyone can be "bumped" or "busted"

Brown paper bags over the head: torture & death

Wipe the mouth away

wipe the eyes away, wipe the ears away, wipe the "long ago" away

A better hand of death will guide you from this hungry ghost world

Gunned down on your own street

Code of executioner's light

Exultant the civvies turned on to torture

Wild laughter getting their kicks in the hungry ghost realm

Set teeth to knuckles

Set knuckles to knees

Set fists to bloated belly

A muzzle snaps

The lights out & they are trashing

Thrashing: metal set to teeth

Set teeth to neck

Hungry ghost: a bloodsuckers paradise

Being sexy again in a broken world, caress the body of the hungry ghost

Chamber of greed & brutality

The ghost that will never rest is your own grasping mind

Cold savage beatings, mannerisms of the thumbs up

A code of hungry ghost is your own mind

Apprehension of the ghost, where next?

Locked doors, low light, agony going down the hallway

Agony in the hit in the stomach "or worse"

Hungry ghost links memory to energy

Atrocity which is silence

Migrations of hungry ghosts walking toward a diminishing hope

Memory erased, women & children disappearing overnight

Hungry ghost an empty verbiage

Sons "disappeared"

Hungry ghost the seer will teach you how to be "ghosted"

Hungry ghost with generations of progeny

Wound that never heals

What perpetuates hungry ghost? coercion without flavor of love?

A culture that flees from love

Hungry ghost an emphatic disruption, a cultural intervention

Achieving power over millions on dark & bloody ground

Simonides: *create a memory system for me lest I forget*

Hungry ghost bursting out of superstitious darkness into Copernican
heliocentricity

Hungry ghost in the half light of memory, lunar memory

Rare native grasses, bed down here, hungry ghost: rest your spectral bones

Riparian habitat: bed down, rest by water: rest your salivating maw

Shadows resting now in the charnel ground of hungry ghost

Preble's jumping mice, coyotes, badgers, coming alive at the toxic nuclear
plant

Swirl of ravens, and vultures hovering nearby in the mind

A line of conifers won't shelter a hungry ghost

A ligament or tendon pulls hard on the phantom bone, no shelter for
hungry ghost

Tiny throat

Distended bloated belly

No comfort for hungry ghost

Hungry ghost, old fracture to haunt you, hungry ghost a crypsis, a
camouflage

Hungry ghost: psychic lockdown

Un-manifest identity without a body

An expansion of unrecognizable things

Phantom memories coiled one upon the other

Hungry ghost without purpose except growing hungrier

Oil! Oil! Oil! Oil!

All you thought in terms of progress vanishes

I awoke one night in the continuous present, we were all wired

Bent over my own body of hungry ghost

Stroked the desire of hungry ghost, stoked the fire of hungry ghost

Nothing but cinder and ashes

Imploding our planet of hungry ghost

餓鬼

餓鬼是佛教輪迴中的六大剎境之一，餓鬼道是一個有實際的飢餓和無法滿足的心理飢餓的地方。對我來説，它象徵著對化石燃料永無止境的需求，以及對我們的星球的破壞。

餓鬼，一種在我們剎境之間的形態

餓鬼：一種永無休止的吞噬世界的意識

性感的鬼，一個表演者，惡魔，牛虻，玩家

從來沒有足夠感覺足夠取得足夠，從來沒有足夠取得足夠感覺足夠

碳鬼！在煤上跳舞

一種心態，為了他想或她想而不滿意，不安心，

為了他們認為他想要甚麼她想要甚麼他們想要甚麼

他者的「我」想和要甚麼：為餓鬼而設的象形
文字！

被波浪沖擊，真的那一種，把你拉了下去。

被水力壓裂的工程沖擊，地震在你腳下

地球説不喜歡不要做不喜歡水力壓裂嘿嘿嘿

湍流在清醒和睡眠之間的影子領域

餓鬼用的犧牲品放在沙地上，粗削的人物畫在洞穴深處，胳膊和腿
使天才之筆充滿生氣，有如電影一般的動物手勢在空間跑步，
在語言中狩獵，手腳亂動，用餓鬼瘦削的筆尖寫作

與餓鬼同眠，他寫作你的末日之書

餓鬼：網絡，電影，小徑，記下潛在的想法，不會放棄

觀者在看你的在你餓鬼的構成

摘下手套，甚麼事都有可能發生

餓鬼，戰爭機器，與嗡嗡作響的戰爭機器同眠

餓鬼，世界之間的一個模糊的殘影，輕彈慾望的細絲，代碼是可以
召喚幻覺的「敵人！敵人！」

我們是敵人

貪得無厭的敵意，一味要油油油！

慾望的線絲一次又一次斷裂，樂器的弦，彈撥，突然折斷

為石油屠殺

為石油流血

唱著哀歌的餓鬼陷於困境

唱著：*我是鬼，我很餓，陷於困境，陷於困境*

有住是渴望的幽靈，

渴望生存，*陷於困境*

渴望生計，*陷於困境*

侏羅紀餓鬼，體型龐大的雜食動物，食慾大的驚人

餓鬼思想古舊，繼承所有原始餓鬼的思維

掠奪和正在掠奪，已經掠奪和將會已經掠奪和將會掠奪和將會已經被掠奪陷於困境陷於困境

壯麗的白光色調到處追趕你，聚光照著慾望

然後那麼明亮或激烈你永遠不能休息

我們究竟怎能餵飽你狼吞虎咽的獵犬？

誘人的慾望色彩光輝燦爛，虛幻的美點綴著你衣衫襤褸的外形

雖然也破爛，短暫的閃爍

經歷了多次今生前世的輪迴，餓鬼

落魄、骯髒，在街上，扣著鐐銬

身體被人翻檢，在街上在「那邊」遙遠的街

餓鬼世界的另一邊

人們願意死在那裏，對抗飢餓的鬼

獨裁者，暴君，傭傭兵，餓鬼世界的居民

星星，原子，分子，名稱家庭歷史，所有都扣上銬鐐

豪里河就在你面前

你的河流封鎖了

恒河封鎖了

長江封鎖了

彎腰走進餓鬼的河

虐待者可以為所欲為

也許任何人都可以被人「幹掉」或「坑了」

棕色的紙袋罩著頭：酷刑和死亡

擦掉嘴巴

擦掉眼睛，擦掉耳朵，擦掉「很久以前」

更好的死亡之手將指引你離開這個餓鬼世界

在自己住的街上被槍殺

劊子手的光的代碼

平民歡喜若狂，要使用酷刑

在餓鬼的領域，狂野的笑聲感到過癮

讓牙齒咬關節

讓關節打膝蓋

讓拳頭打腫脹的肚子

一枝槍口突然斷裂

燈關掉了，他們在扔垃圾

鞭打：讓金屬敲打牙齒

讓牙齒咬頸部

餓鬼：吸血鬼的樂園

在破碎的世界裏再度性感，

愛撫餓鬼的身體

貪念和暴行的房間

永無休止的鬼就是你自己貪婪的心

冷酷無情，野蠻毒打，舉起大拇指的言談舉止

餓鬼的代碼就是你自己的心

鬼的憂慮，下一次在哪裏？

鎖著的門，暗淡的光，創痛沿著長廊走下

肚子被打的痛楚，可有「或更糟的事情」

餓鬼把記憶與能源連接起來

沉默是暴行

餓鬼遷移，走向不斷遞減的希望

記憶抹去了，婦女和兒童在一夜之間消失

餓鬼沒意義的廢話

兒子們「消失」

餓鬼先知者會教你如何「鬼化」

餓鬼有一代又一代的子孫

永遠不會癒合的傷口

為甚麼餓鬼可以歷久不衰？強迫而沒有愛的意味？

離愛而去的文化

餓鬼強勢的擾亂，文化干預

在數百萬人的黑暗和血腥的地上取得權力

西蒙尼戴斯：*為我創建一個記憶系統，唯恐我忘記*

餓鬼衝破迷信的黑暗，走進哥白尼體系的太陽中心論

餓鬼在記憶的半光半暗之中，月球的記憶

罕見的本地草坪，在這裏鋪牀睡覺，餓鬼：讓你的幽靈骨頭休息

河邊的棲息地：鋪牀睡覺，在水邊休息：讓你垂涎欲滴的食慾休息

陰影正在餓鬼的停屍地上休息

冒充者的跳鼠，郊狼，獾，在有毒的核電站變得很有生氣

烏鴉打圈，心裏的禿鷹在附近盤旋

一行針葉樹不能庇護餓鬼

一條韌帶或肌腱使勁地拔鬼怪的骨頭，餓鬼沒有庇護所

微小的喉嚨

膨脹浮腫的肚子

沒有給餓鬼帶來安慰

餓鬼，骨折舊患纏擾你，餓鬼一種保護色、一種迷彩

餓鬼：心靈封鎖

未曾顯示的身份沒有身體

無法辨認東西的擴展

幻影記憶一個又一個的盤繞疊起

餓鬼沒有目的，除了越來越飢餓

石油！石油！石油！石油！

你有關發展的想法全部都消失了

有一天晚上，我在持續的現在醒來，我們全都有連線

彎下我餓鬼的身子

撫摸餓鬼的慾望撥餓鬼的火

除了煤渣和灰燼甚麼都沒有

我們這餓鬼的星球內爆

（方梓勳、陳嘉恩　譯）

王小妮，曾任海南大學教授。出版有詩集《我的紙裏包著我的火》、《半個我正在疼痛》、《有甚麼在我心裏一過》(香港中文大學出版社，2014)、《致另一個世界》，《出門種葵花》，《月光79首》。另出版有小說隨筆多部。

Wang Xiaoni has taught at Hainan University. Her poetry publications include *My Paper Wraps My Fire*, *Something Crosses My Mind*, and *To Another World*. The translation of her book *Something Crosses My Mind* (The Chinese University Press, 2014) by Eleanor Goodman was shortlisted for the Griffin Poetry Prize in 2015.

王小妮

WANG XIAONI

致晴天

天這麼好，而我這麼不好。

迷路的雲彩
騎大灰馬的雲彩
金鑰匙一樣的飛機描著更金的邊兒。
這是哪一個人間
是你們的還是我的。
這麼奇幻的天布都敢掛出來
還一定要我看見。

在兩個世界間穿梭的是燒燙的鐵
未來的蒼白和冰涼
就等著那鑽頭的刺啦一聲。

To a Sunny Day

The day is so nice, but I'm not.

Lost clouds
clouds riding a big gray horse
and the gold key of an airplane tracing a golden border.
Whose world is this
yours or mine.
The fantastical sky dares to drape itself down
to make sure I see it.

Burning iron shuttles between these two worlds
the future's pallidness and cold
wait for that whirring stab of the drill bit.

(Translated by Eleanor Goodman)

致蹲下去看魚的人

我的學生在看魚
看肚子朝上的幾個還有沒有呼吸。

藥片大的不蠕動的紅嘴唇
鉛墜，小刀，指甲鉗。
流水很驚悚
牠們死後都會跳起來的
看那光
六月的太陽像針刺。

To the Person Crouching to Look at Fish

My student is looking at the fish,
looking at their bellies to see if any are still breathing.

Lozenge-sized unmoving red mouths
plummet, pocket knife, fingernail clipper.
The water is startled
after they die they'll leap up
to see the light
and the June sun will be just like acupuncture.

(Translated by Eleanor Goodman)

致雷雨

多餘的人都要被收回去。
天在摸黑點名
這儀式需要隆重
轟轟烈烈丟盔卸甲。

玻璃拍著太脆的心
早知道有這麼一夜。
天上就要滿了
抬頭見到的都是熟人。
閃電蹦出來，露一下笑臉
這麼多的激情滿街亂串，最享受了。

To a Thunderstorm

All the superfluous people will be gathered back in.
The sky calls roll in the dark
and the ceremony has to be grandiose
with every single thing being tossed into headlong flight.

Glass beats with a brittle heart
have long known such a night would come.
The sky is almost full
and everyone seen up there is familiar.
Lightning whips out, revealing a smile
fervor and chaos in the streets, what it likes most.

(Translated by Eleanor Goodman)

致投在教室天花板上的銀河

聽說這就是銀河
下面發出讚歎。
有人衝過去拉窗簾
幾幅布使這教室獨立於世
每人每兩只眼睛閃閃發亮呢
我們這些星星。

太小太密的斑點
一大團鳥努力飛進了沒有。
四周都是天牆
某教室裏微微有光的這幾十個。

靜死了，有那麼一小會兒
因為重新看見自己
張著嘴巴吃驚。

To the Milky Way Projected on a Classroom Ceiling

Some say this is the Milky Way
and from below come cries of admiration.
Someone rushes to close the curtains
and strips of cloth set the classroom apart from the world
with our sparkling eyes
we become stars.

The spots are so small and close
has a flock of birds tried to fly between them?
Around us are heavenly walls
and dozens of faint lights dotting the classroom.

It's quiet as death, and after a moment
we see ourselves anew
mouths dropping open in surprise.

(Translated by Eleanor Goodman)

致京郊的煙囱

天上最空蕩的地方
高大的煙囱正噴出濃煙。
滔滔不絕的黑卷髮
北方姑娘那根粗壯的獨辮子。
濃密又翻滾
蠻不講理地甩出去
正在氣頭上的灰姑娘。

誰也不能説服她回家
那惡霸一樣的水泥煙囱是她爸爸。
憤怒在推她，跑向更大的灰幕
她要站起來嗎
她這是要頂破天嗎。

To the Chimneys in Suburban Beijing

In the emptiest spot in the sky
tall chimneys spurt out thick smoke.
The endlessly winding black twist
of a northern girl's thick braid.
Dense and billowing
and raging it spits out
Cinderella on a puff of smoke.

No one can convince her to go home
that tyrant of a chimney is her father.
Anger goads her toward a larger ash curtain
will she stand up
will she break through the sky?

(Translated by Eleanor Goodman)

致灰霾

一個個路人都鑽過來了
能看見推車人臉上的皺紋
哦，那可真像一張抽巴的狀子。

終於來到了近前
汽車前窗貼著蜜蜂們折斷的翅膀。
努力讓自己顯出來
誰也不想就這樣被埋沒。

謝謝這混沌的末日
讓我發現每一個微小可愛是怎樣掙脱的。
寶寶緊兜在前心
那個有辮子的小媽媽還能念兒歌
我的天哦。

To Gray Haze

Walkers burrow in one by one
wrinkles on the face of a man pushing a cart
look like a crumpled-up petition.

Finally making it through
a windshield is covered with broken honeybee wings.
It tries to show itself again
since no one wants to be buried that way.

I'm grateful to that chaotic doomsday
for showing me how each lovable thing gets cast off.
A baby cradled tight to the chest
of a young mother in braids—she can still sing nursery rhymes
for heaven's sake.

(Translated by Eleanor Goodman)

致黃昏的黃鼠狼

瓦片響得很近，像頸椎骨響。
夜晚緩慢地圍捕過來
一個也不放過。
而竹林間忽然蕩過金毛
那一閃
在我眼前就是飛了。

預言應驗的季節
稻田立起葉尖的黃刺。
就在太陽只剩下半個的那瞬間
唿哨的黃鼠狼穿屋而過
跟著一枚銅箭
疼哦，四下裏終於死一樣的黑。

For a Weasel at Dusk

Tiles rattle nearby, like vertebrae clicking.
The evening slowly surrounds us
and won't let anything get away.
But golden fur suddenly flashes in the bamboo forest
and something
flits past my eyes.

In this predicted season
rice paddies are filled with yellow thorn tips.
As soon as only half of the sun is left
a whistling weasel crosses by the cabin
chasing a copper arrow
and oh it hurts, everything covered in deathly darkness.

(Translated by Eleanor Goodman)

致接電話的

鄉下的狗叫
一定來了陌生人。
大晌午，忽然有手機在唱〈東方紅〉
這時候狗已經不叫
大家一起聽。

唱到大救星
一個人大聲接電話。
扛著大卷的自來水管
肩膀上環繞著白蛇一樣。
歌就斷在這會兒
改裝自來水的工人一邊罵人一邊爬坡。
哦，剛唱到就斷了。

2009–2014

To the One Taking a Call

Dogs bark in the village
which means a stranger is coming.
At midday, a cell phone suddenly sings "The East Is Red"
the dogs have stopped barking
and everyone listens together.

The lyrics get to the great liberator
and someone answers the phone loudly.
He's carrying a huge water pipe
around his shoulders like a white snake.
The song is interrupted there
and the worker refitting the pipes walks uphill cursing.
Oh, for the song to end there.

2009–2014

(Translated by Eleanor Goodman)

加桑・扎克坦，巴勒斯坦詩人、小説家和編輯，生於伯利恆市附近的貝特賈拉鎮，曾居於約旦、貝魯特、大馬士革及突尼斯，現居巴勒斯坦拉姆安拉市。扎克坦曾出版11本詩集，其中《牠像稻草鳥一樣跟著我》（菲迪・祖達譯）曾獲得2013年格里芬詩歌獎，同年6月獲巴勒斯坦總統頒予國家榮譽勛章，以誌扎克坦對阿拉伯及巴勒斯坦文學的建樹與貢獻；同年秋又獲得諾貝爾文學獎提名，呼聲甚高。扎克坦曾入選奧克拉荷馬大學頒發2014紐斯塔特國際文學獎（該獎被譽為美國的諾貝爾獎）與2015謝赫・扎耶德文學獎。扎克坦的詩給翻譯成多國語言，包括英文、法文、意大利文、挪威文和德文等。2000至2004年間，扎克坦曾擔任詩刊《Al-Shoua'ra》的主編，也是「詩歌之家」的主任，現為福利委員會文化政策顧問，以及馬赫曼德・達爾維什基金會執委會會員。扎克坦亦為《Al-Ayyam》和《Emirate 24》寫專欄，同時又是《敘述巴勒斯坦》文化季刊的主編。其父卡里爾・扎克坦也是詩人。

Ghassan Zaqtan is a Palestinian poet, novelist, and editor. He is author of eleven collections of poetry. Born in Beit Jala, near Bethlehem, he has lived in Jordan, Beirut, Damascus, and Tunis, and currently resides in Ramallah. His book *Like a Straw Bird It Follows Me,* translated by Fady Joudah was awarded the Griffin Poetry Prize in 2013. In recognition of his achievement and contribution to Arabic and Palestinian literature, Ghassan Zaqtan was awarded the National Medal of Honor by the Palestinian president in June the same year. He was also nominated among the short-listed winners of the 2014 Neustadt International Prize for Literature, an award sponsored by the University of Oklahoma and perceived as the American equivalent for the Nobel Prize for Literature, and the 2015 Sheikh Zayid Literature Prize. His name appeared for the first time in the fall of 2013 on the speculation list for the Nobel Prize for Literature. His work has been translated into English, French, Italian, Norwegian, German and other languages. He was the editor of *Al-Shoua'ra* from 2000 to 2004 and director of the House of Poetry. He is also a consultant for cultural policies in the Welfare Association and a member of the executive board of the Mahmoud Darwish Foundation. He writes a weekly column in the *Al-Ayyam* newspaper and *Emirate 24*, and is the editor of the quarterly cultural magazine *Palestinian Narrative*. His father, Khalil Zaqtan, was also a poet.

加桑 · 扎克坦

GHASSAN ZAQTAN

مخدّة

هل ظلَّ وَقتُ كي أَقولَ لها:
مساءُ الخيرِ يا أُمّي
رَجعتُ بطلقَةٍ في القلب
تلكَ مَخدَّتي،
وَأُريدُ أَن أَرتاح.
قولي:
إِنَّهُ يَرتاحُ
لو دقَّتْ علينا الحرب.

枕頭

時間是否還足夠我對她說：
晚上好啊，媽媽
我回來了，一顆子彈中了心臟。
那是我的枕頭，
我想好好歇息。
告訴別人：
他在休息
即便戰爭已叩響我們的門。

（唐珺　譯）

A Pillow

Is there time left
for me to say to her
Good evening Mom
I'm back
with a bullet in my heart
and that's my pillow
I want to rest.

And Mom
if war knocks
say
he's taking a rest

(Translated by Fady Joudah)

الموتى في الحديقة

لا تفتحي الشبّاكْ
لا تستيقظي
أرجوكِ،لا تستيقظي
كانوا على عشبِ الحديقةِ يرقصونَ

كأنّهم سببُ الحديقةِ
أو تأمُّلها
وكانوا يصرخونَ هناكْ.

تحتَ الضوءِ
كان غبارُهمْ ينحلّ.

كانت أمطرتْ في الليلِ،
طول الليلْ.

公園裏的死者

不要開窗
不要醒來
求求你，不要醒來
他們在公園的草地上舞蹈
像是公園的理由
或是它的沉思
他們在那裏嘶喊。

光芒下
他們的塵土在分解。

夜裏下著雨，
一整夜地下。

(唐珺　譯)

The Dead in the Garden

Don't open the window
don't wake up
I beg you don't wake up…
they were dancing on the garden grass
as if they were the garden's motive
or its contemplation
and they were screaming there

beneath the light
their dust was coming apart

it had rained at night
all night

(Translated by Fady Joudah)

عدو يهبط التلال

حين يهبط
أو يُرى هابطاً
حين يوحي لنا أنَّه يهبطُ الآنَ.

التمهلُ والصمتُ
نقصانُه كاملاً
وهو يصغي أمامَ النباتاتْ.
ريبتهُ وهو يهبطُ
المؤجَّلُ من صمته
من أنّهُ ليسَ "نحنُ"
وليسَ "هنا"
يبدأُ الموتْ.

اشترى زهرةً
زهرةً، ليسَ إلاّ،
لا وصايا لها أو إناء.

من التلِّ يمكُن أنْ يُبصرَ الحاجزَ العسكريَ، جنودَ المظلاتِ،
أنْ يبصرَ القاطنينَ، حوافَ الجبالِ، الطريقَ الوحيدةَ
حيثُ ستتركَ أقدامُهم أثراً في الصَخورِ وفي الطينِ والماءْ.

الخساراتُ، أيضاً، ستبدو من التلِّ
متروكةً دونَ جهدٍ.

الهشاشةُ في الظِلِّ
حيثُ اليهوديُّ ذو الشاربينِ ،
الذي يشبهُ العربَ الميّتينَ هَنا.

في حوافِ الجبال، ستبدو الكهوفُ مسالمةً كلُّها
والطريقُ على حالها.

بينما كانَ يهبطُ
كانت كهوفُ الجبالِ تواصل تحديقَها
وهيَ ترمشُ في البَرد.

墜落山下的敵人

當他在墜落
或是看上去在墜落
當他示意我們他正在墜落

從容、靜默
他的殘缺是完整的，
他正面朝草木聆聽。
疑懼伴著他墜落
墜落因其沉默而延遲，
因其不是「我們」、
不是「此地」而延遲。
死亡開始。

他買下一朵花
只是，一朵花，
它沒有遺囑，也沒有花瓶。

從山上，他能看見軍事關卡、看見傘兵，
看見住戶、山崖、唯一的通道，
人們將會留下足跡，在岩石、泥土和水中。

同樣地，他能看見損失
像是被匆匆遺留在山上。

他看見模糊的背影，
那留著兩撇髭鬚的猶太人，
一如長眠此地的阿拉伯人。

山崖上，所有洞穴都顯得安全，
通道一如既往。

在他墜落的同時
山洞繼續它們的注視，
在冷冽中眨眼。

(唐珺　譯)

An Enemy Comes Down the Hill

When he comes down
or is seen coming down
when he reveals to us that he is coming down.

Waiting and silence

his entire lack
when he hearkens before the plants.

His caution when he comes down
like one postponed by his quiet
by his being not "us"
and not "here"
death begins.

He bought a flower
a flower, nothing more,
that has no vase and leaves no will.

From the hill the military checkpoint can be seen, the paratroopers…
those who squat can be seen, the edges of mountains, and the only road…
where their feet will leave a trace in the rocks, mud, and water.

Losses also will appear from the hill
abandoned without effort.

And the fragility in shadow,
where the Jewish man with a long mustache,
the one who resembles the dead Arabs here:
from the mountain edges, all the caves will appear peaceful
and the road as it were.

While he was coming down
the mountain caves continued to stare
and blink in the cold.

(Translated by Fady Joudah)

أغنيةُ الكرم

يا ابنتي
عندما تذهبين لقطفِ السفرجلِ
لا توقظيني

أنا ميتُ منذُ وقتٍ طويلٍ، كما تعرفين،
أنامُ على حجرٍ باردٍ مثلَ صيفٍ قديم
تُقلّبُني الشمسُ ذاتَ اليمينِ وذاتَ الشّمالِ
وتنقرُ رأسي العصافير.

مررَّني الضوءُ للظلِّ
والظلُّ للضوءِ.

كانت لغاتُ العبيدِ ولهجاتُهم تملأُ الليلَ
لمّا عبرتُ،
وكانتْ تعاويذهُم تُمسكُ الذكرياتِ
وتَسحبُها خلفهُم مثلَ نملٍ كثيفٍ

وكانت دفوفُ المغنّينَ تسبحُ كالطوفِ حولَ الشعاعِ
وترفعُني في هواءٍ سعيدٍ

وكنتُ على حافةِ الكرمِ، كرم السفرجلِ،
أقرأُ روميّةً، ربما، للأميرِ الأَسيرِ:

فليتك تصفو...

果園的歌

女兒啊
當你要去採摘榅桲
不要叫醒我

我已死去很久，如你所知，
我睡在一塊冰冷的岩石上，如同一段舊夏
擁有左與右的太陽親吻著我
飛鳥啄著我的頭

光把我傳給影
影把我傳給光。

在我途經時，
奴隸的語言和方言充斥了黑夜
他們的咒語將記憶緊緊抓住
牽在身後，像密集的蟻群

歌者們的手鼓漂遊著，像圍著光線繞圈
將我高升至幸福的空氣裏

我在果園邊——榅桲樹園邊，
正讀著《羅馬集》[1]，也許，讀給被俘的王子：

惟願你歡愉……

(唐珺　譯)

譯註：

1. 十世紀阿拉伯哈姆丹王朝「王子詩人」艾布・菲拉斯・哈姆達尼所作，他出征拜占庭被俘後在獄中寫下《羅馬集》。

The Orchard Song

Dear daughter
when you go to pick the quince
don't wake me

I've been dead for a long time, as you know,
like an ancient summer I sleep on a cold stone
the sun turns me to the right and to the left
and the birds peck my head

Light passed me to shadow
shadow to light

...and the languages and dialects of slaves
used to fill the night when I passed,
and their amulets held the memories
and dragged them as if a swarm of ants

The singers' tambourines were swimming like a raft
around the radiance,
lifting me in a joyous air
and I was by the orchard's edge, the quince orchard,
reading an ode, perhaps by the captive prince:

I wish you'd turn serene...

(Translated by Fady Joudah)

出版 Publisher

香港中文大學出版社 The Chinese University Press

封面影像 Cover Image

北島 Bei Dao

封面設計 Cover Design

麥安 Ann Mak

出版日期 Date of Publication

二零一五年十一月 November 2015

國際書號 ISBN

978-962-996-721-5

Printed in Hong Kong

中文大學出版社
THE CHINESE UNIVERSITY PRESS
www.chineseupress.com
HONG KONG, CHINA

香港國際詩歌之夜2015
International Poetry Nights in Hong Kong 2015

主辦單位 Organizer

香港中文大學文學院 Faculty of Arts, The Chinese University of Hong Kong

協辦單位 Co-organizers

香港中文大學中國文化研究所
Institute of Chinese Studies, The Chinese University of Hong Kong
香港中文大學出版社 The Chinese University Press
香港兆基創意書院 HKICC Lee Shau Kee School of Creativity
廣州時刻文化傳播有限公司 Moment Communications

贊助 Sponsors

香港法國文化協會 Alliance Française de Hong Kong
上海廿一文化發展有限公司 Shanghai 21 Culture Promotion Co., Ltd.
中國會 The China Club
香港文學出版社有限公司 The Hong Kong Literary Press Co. Limited
斑馬谷文化發展(北京)有限公司 Zebra Valley Culture Development